STAR WARS™

CHARACTER ENCYCLOPEDIA

UPDATED AND
EXPANDED

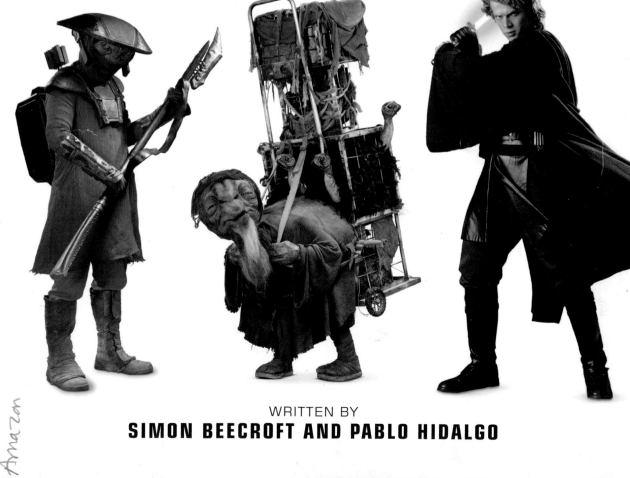

WRITTEN BY
SIMON BEECROFT AND PABLO HIDALGO

CONTENTS

Who planned the rebel assault on the first Death Star? Which surly alien lost an arm in a Mos Eisley cantina? The *Star Wars* galaxy is full of heroes, villains, aliens, creatures, and droids. All have played their part—large or small—in the events of the dying days of the Galactic Republic, the battles of the Clone Wars, the desperate rebellion against the Empire, and the rise of the First Order.

FINDING A CHARACTER

Look up characters alphabetically by their first name or title or use the index on page 222

2-1B

SURGICAL DROID

DATA FILE

AFFILIATION: None
TYPE: Surgical droid
MANUFACTURER:
Industrial Automaton
HEIGHT: 1.77m (5ft 10in)
APPEARANCES: CW,
III, V, VI
SEE ALSO:
FX-series droid

Vocabulator

Hypodermic injector

Transparent shell over hydraulics

2-1B MEDICAL and surgical droids have been around since Republic times. One such unit is attached to the rebel base on Hoth. He treats the injuries of many rebel troops, including Luke Skywalker after a wampa attacks him.

SURGICAL DROIDS in the 2-1B series are equipped with encyclopedic memory banks. They ensure that the droids give the best course of treatment in any medical situation.

A Republic-era 2-1B droid rebuilds Darth Vader's burned body.

Hydraulic leg

Stabilizing foot

Rebel Surgeon

2-1B is able to perform extremely precise operations that leave little or no scar. The droid's long experience with humans makes him a caring medic. Luke Skywalker is so impressed with 2-1B's skills, he requests that the droid treat him again after he loses his hand on Cloud City.

4-LOM

DATA FILE

AFFILIATION: Bounty hunter
TYPE: LOM-series protocol droid
MANUFACTURER: Industrial Automaton
HEIGHT: 1.67m (5ft 6in)
APPEARANCES: V
SEE ALSO: Zuckuss; Jabba the Hutt; Darth Vader

Compound photoreceptors

After the Battle of Hoth, Vader hires 4-LOM and others to locate the *Millennium Falcon*.

THIS HUMANOID DROID with an insect-like face used to be a sophisticated protocol droid made to resemble the species he served. 4-LOM was once assigned to a luxury liner, but he overwrote his own programming and began a life of crime as a bounty hunter.

BlasTech DLT-19 heavy blaster rifle

Battered black droid plating

THE PERSONALITY

software corruption that transformed 4-LOM into a deadly bounty hunter is a known flaw in the LOM-series. Other similarly affected protocol droids of the same make have been spotted working as enforcers in the Outer Rim Territories.

Dangerous Duo

4-LOM often works in partnership with a bounty hunter named Zuckuss. The combination of 4-LOM's powers of deduction and analysis with Zuckuss's mystical intuition makes their collaboration successful and lucrative.

AAYLA SECURA

TWI'LEK JEDI KNIGHT

DATA FILE

AFFILIATION: Jedi
HOMEWORLD: Ryloth
SPECIES: Twi'lek
HEIGHT: 1.7m (5ft 7in)
APPEARANCES: II, CW, III
SEE ALSO: Kit Fisto; Mace Windu; Yoda

Has mastered Ataru, Form IV of lightsaber combat

Lekku (head-tail)

Djem So attack stance

CUNNING AAYLA SECURA is a Twi'lek Jedi Knight who relies on her athletic lightsaber skills to outwit opponents. As a Jedi General, Aayla leads a squad of clone troopers on many campaigns.

AAYLA SECURA is an intelligent, sometimes mischievous Jedi. Her teacher was a troubled Jedi named Quinlan Vos. Aayla passes on the teachings of her Master to young Ahsoka Tano during a Clone Wars mission that goes awry and ends up on the grassland planet of Maridun.

Belt made of rycrit hide

Fitted clothing allows complete freedom of movement

Secura's own clone troopers turn on her on Felucia.

Captured

At the Battle of Geonosis, Aayla Secura is among the circle of Jedi captured by Geonosian soldiers. Luckily, clone trooper reinforcements come to their rescue.

ACKLAY

GEONOSIS ARENA BEASTS

DATA FILE

HOMEWORLD: Vendaxa
HEIGHT: 3.05m (10ft)
DIET: Carnivorous
HABITAT: Underwater, land
APPEARANCES: II
SEE ALSO: Nexu; reek;
Obi-Wan Kenobi

CONDEMNED PRISONERS IN the Geonosis execution arenas face certain death by wild beasts. Many of these creatures are caught and transported to Geonosis from their home planets far away. The ferocious acklay is one of these exotic beasts.

Hardened, skin-covered claw

Razor-sharp teeth

Acklays walk on long, clawed fingertips.

THE ACKLAY'S homeworld is a fertile planet named Vendaxa. They live underwater but emerge to hunt on the plains for creatures named lemnai.

Grappling hand

Stretchy stomach

Protective bony nodules

Acklay Attack
Jedi Obi-Wan Kenobi uses a Geonosian picador's pike to defend himself against the savage acklay's onslaught.

ADI GALLIA

THOLOTHIAN JEDI MASTER

DATA FILE

AFFILIATION: Jedi
HOMEWORLD: Coruscant
SPECIES: Tholothian
HEIGHT: 1.84m (6ft)
APPEARANCES: I, II, CW
SEE ALSO: Stass Allie; Even Piell; Chancellor Valorum; Bail Organa

JEDI MASTER ADI GALLIA was born into a high-ranking diplomatic family stationed on Coruscant. Gallia is a Jedi High Council member and a noble General in the Clone Wars.

Long, fleshy tendrils descend from scaled cranium

Jedi robe

Lightsaber

Utility pouch

As a High Council member, Adi Gallia is respected for her powers of intuition.

Tall travel boots

ADI GALLIA was a valuable intelligence source to Senate leaders. Her life was cut short in the Clone Wars when she was killed by the renegade Sith apprentice, Savage Opress.

Jedi Temple

Gallia may be stationed at the Jedi Temple on Coruscant, but she is finely attuned to events farther afield. Gallia is the first to warn the Senate of the Trade Federation's suspicious activity in the Naboo System.

ADMIRAL ACKBAR

RESISTANCE SPACE FORCE ADMIRAL

DATA FILE

AFFILIATION: Rebel Alliance/ Resistance
HOMEWORLD: Mon Cala
SPECIES: Mon Calamari
HEIGHT: 1.8m (5ft 11in)
APPEARANCES: CW, VI, VII
SEE ALSO: Lando Calrissian; Mon Mothma; General Madine; Princess Leia

ADMIRAL ACKBAR was born on the ocean world of Mon Cala. A veteran of the Clone Wars, Ackbar is later instrumental in bringing his people into the Rebel Alliance. After the Galactic Civil War, he is coaxed out of retirement by Princess Leia to join the Resistance during the rise of the First Order.

Rank badge

Waterproof skin

Belt clasp

Ackbar commanded the rebel fleet from his personal flagship, *Home One*.

AS COMMANDER

of the rebel fleet, Admiral Ackbar planned and led the attack on the Empire's capital ships at the Battle of Endor.

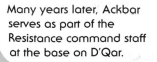

Many years later, Ackbar serves as part of the Resistance command staff at the base on D'Qar.

Home One

Ackbar's people contributed their giant Mon Cal star cruisers to the Alliance. *Home One* served as a mobile command center after the Empire discovered and destroyed the main Alliance headquarters on Hoth.

ADMIRAL OZZEL

ADMIRAL OF THE *EXECUTOR*

DATA FILE

AFFILIATION: Empire
HOMEWORLD: Carida
SPECIES: Human
HEIGHT: 1.75m (5ft 9in)
APPEARANCES: V
SEE ALSO: Admiral Piett;
General Veers; Darth Vader

Officer's disk

Imperial code cylinder

Rank insignia plaque

Belt buckle contains secret data-storage compartment

KENDEL OZZEL is the commander of Darth Vader's gigantic flagship, the *Executor.* Under Ozzel's sometimes uncertain command, the *Executor* emerges from hyperspace too close to Hoth, alerting the rebels to the Imperials' presence.

KENDAL OZZEL

serves in the Republic Navy during the Clone Wars and soon works his way up the military ladder. Ozzel is ambitious but displays poor judgment and ineffective tactical thinking, which he attempts to mask with his authoritarian persona.

The *Executor* leads Darth Vader's personal fleet of Star Destroyers, known as Death Squadron.

Durasteel-toed boots

Deadly Blunders

Vader's view of Ozzel is that he is "as clumsy as he is stupid." After a series of blunders by Ozzel—first, doubting evidence of life on Hoth, then the failed attempt to surprise the rebels—Vader force-chokes Ozzel and promotes Captain Piett to Admiral in Ozzel's place.

ADMIRAL PIETT

COMMANDER OF THE *EXECUTOR*

DATA FILE

AFFILIATION: Empire
HOMEWORLD: Axxila
SPECIES: Human
HEIGHT: 1.73m (5ft 8in)
APPEARANCES: V, VI
SEE ALSO: Admiral Ozzel;
Darth Vader

An A-wing destroys the *Executor*'s bridge crew and causes the ship to crash.

PIETT IS A LOYAL IMPERIAL captain on Darth Vader's flagship, the *Executor*. After Vader Force-chokes Admiral Ozzel to death for incompetence, Piett is instantly promoted to Admiral of the fleet. Piett loses his life when a rebel A-wing crashes through the bridge of the *Executor*.

Naval officer's tunic

Leather gloves

UNLIKE MOST Imperial officers, who come from the prestigious Inner Core worlds, Firmus Piett has his origins in in the Outer Rim. He is known for his quick thinking, as well as his ability to shift blame for mistakes he has made.

Risky Strategy

Vader's officers must submit entirely to the Dark Lord's iron will. When Vader insists that Piett makes a risky pursuit of the *Millennium Falcon* into an asteroid field, Piett nervously does Vader's bidding, aware that errors could lead to his death.

ADMIRAL STATURA

RESISTANCE OFFICER

DATA FILE

AFFILIATION: Resistance
HOMEWORLD: Garel
SPECIES: Human
HEIGHT: 1.72m (5ft 8in)
APPEARANCES: VII
SEE ALSO: Princess Leia;
Admiral Ackbar; Major
Ematt; Major Brance

STATURA WAS ONLY a teenager when the war against the Galactic Empire ended, but he experienced combat firsthand while trying to liberate his homeworld from Imperial rule. He loyally serves General Leia Organa.

Repurposed Rebel Alliance crest

Admiral's rank badge

WHEN GENERAL Organa assembled trusted military advisors to form the core of her Resistance movement, she turned to experienced rebel veterans. Statura was younger than most, and plucked from a career in applied sciences.

Statura watches the battle above the Starkiller unfold from the Resistance command center on D'Qar.

Battle Analysis

Statura is practical and technically minded, traits he uses well in his role supervising logistics for the Resistance. He keenly assesses the Starkiller threat, correctly guessing the unimaginable scale of its destructive power. It is his analysis that leads to the Resistance starfighter attack on the weapon.

AGEN KOLAR

ZABRAK JEDI MASTER

DATA FILE

AFFILIATION: Jedi
HOMEWORLD: Coruscant
SPECIES: Zabrak
HEIGHT: 1.9m (6ft 4in)
APPEARANCES: II, III
SEE ALSO: Mace Windu;
Saesee Tiin; Kit Fisto

Horns
regenerate
over time

Lightsaber uses duel
crystals to create green
or blue energy blades

Two-handed
ready stance

AGEN KOLAR is a
Zabrak, as is fellow Jedi Eeth
Koth. The Zabrak species is
identified by its head horns.
Known to strike first and ask
questions later, Kolar is also
a valuable member of the
Jedi High Council.

AGEN KOLAR is
a master swordsmith
who joins the 200 Jedi
Knights that battle the
Separatist army on
Geonosis. Mace Windu
has a high opinion of
Kolar's combat skills,
and enlists him in a
desperate attempt
to arrest Supreme
Chancellor Palpatine.

Hooded robe often
removed in combat

Agen Kolar's renowned lightsaber
skills are put to use on Geonosis.

Skillful Sith

Even the celebrated sword skills
of Agen Kolar cannot match the
speed and unsparing power of
a Sith Lord such as Darth Sidious.

ANAKIN SKYWALKER

LEGENDARY JEDI KNIGHT

Gauntlet covers mechno-hand
(which replaces hand sliced
off by Count Dooku)

DATA FILE

AFFILIATION: Podracing, Jedi, Sith
HOMEWORLD: Tatooine
SPECIES: Human
HEIGHT: 1.85m (6ft 1in)
APPEARANCES: I, II, CW, III, VI
SEE ALSO: Qui-Gon Jinn; Obi-Wan Kenobi; Padmé Amidala

Jedi utility belt

Young Anakin's keen perception and unnaturally fast reflexes show his great Force potential.

IN THE CLONE WARS,
Anakin loses his faith in the Jedi to restore peace and harmony to the galaxy. He also feels great anger at the tragic death of his mother and fears that the same fate may befall Padmé Amidala (who is secretly his wife). Finally, Anakin is persuaded that only the dark side can give him the power to prevent death.

ANAKIN SKYWALKER'S rise to power is astonishing. In a few short years, he goes from being a slave on Tatooine to becoming one of the most powerful Jedi ever. But Anakin's thirst for power leads him to the dark side of the Force, with tragic consequences for the galaxy.

Anakin's impulsive nature leads him toward the dark side.

Close Bond
Anakin's bond with his teacher, Obi-Wan Kenobi, is strong. They make a dynamic team in the Clone Wars, where Anakin proves to be a great leader. Yet Anakin is troubled by feelings of anger and mistrust.

AT-AT PILOT

DATA FILE

AFFILIATION: Empire
SPECIES: Human
AVERAGE HEIGHT:
1.83m (6ft)
STANDARD EQUIPMENT:
Blaster pistol; thermal
detonators; grenades
APPEARANCES: R, V,
SEE ALSO: AT-ST pilot;
General Veers

ONLY THE STRONGEST Imperial soldiers are put forward for training to become pilots of the terrifying All Terrain Armored Transport (AT-AT) walkers. AT-AT pilots, who generally work in pairs, consider themselves all-powerful.

Reinforced helmet

Life-support pack

Insulated jumpsuit

AT-ATs are not climate controlled, so pilots wear special insulated suits on frozen planets such as Hoth. The suits protect the wearer if the walker's pressurized cockpit is smashed open in hostile environments.

Driving gauntlet

The pilots sit in the cockpit in the AT-AT's head, operating driving and firing controls.

Walking Terror
The giant AT-AT walkers march relentlessly across uneven battlegrounds, using their mighty laser cannons to wreak destruction on the enemy forces below.

AT-ST PILOT

IMPERIAL SCOUT WALKER CREW

DATA FILE

AFFILIATION: Empire

SPECIES: Human

STANDARD EQUIPMENT:
Blasters; grenades; thermal detonators; emergency flares; comlink

APPEARANCES: V, VI

SEE ALSO: AT-AT pilot; Chewbacca

AT-STs are equipped with two powerful medium blaster cannons.

Jumpsuit

AT-ST PILOTS
wear open-face helmets, blast goggles, and basic armor plating underneath their jumpsuits. In the Battle of Endor, AT-ST walkers are deployed against the rebels. Many are lost to surprise attacks by Ewoks.

TWO-LEGGED AT-ST
(All Terrain Scout Transport) walkers march into battle, spraying blaster bolts at enemy troops. Each walker houses two highly trained pilots with superior skills of balance and agility.

Fire-resistant gauntlet

Two pilots keep the AT-ST walker moving at speed through uneven terrain.

On the Hunt
AT-ST walkers are used on reconnaissance and anti-personnel hunting missions. They are not invulnerable to attack, as Chewbacca demonstrates when he forces his way inside a walker through the roof.

AURRA SING

VICIOUS BOUNTY HUNTER

DATA FILE

AFFILIATION: Bounty hunter
HOMEWORLD: Nar Shaddaa
SPECIES: Human
HEIGHT: 1.83m (6ft)
APPEARANCES: I, CW
SEE ALSO: Bossk; Padmé
Amidala; Boba Fett

AURRA SING is a ruthless bounty hunter. A seemingly ageless veteran of the underworld scene, Aurra worked with such contemporaries as Jango Fett, and Cad Bane. During the Clone Wars, she was hired by Ziro the Hutt to assassinate Padmé Amidala.

Tracker utility vest

Short-range pistol

Long fingers to draw blood

AURRA SING was born in the polluted urban sprawl of Nar Shaddaa. She never knew her father and her mother was too poor to raise her. Sing became a cold-blooded killer. She is willing to use any means necessary to locate her prey. She has sensor implants and has a wide assortment of weapons in her private arsenal, including lightsabers and a sniper's projectile rifle.

Long-range projectile rifle

During the Clone Wars, Aurra guides the recently orphaned Boba Fett.

High Alert

On the trail of her quarry on Tatooine, Aurra Sing is a spectator at the Podrace that will earn young Anakin Skywalker his freedom.

17

A-WING PILOT

DATA FILE

AFFILIATION: Rebel Alliance
SQUADRON NAMES: Phoenix Squadron, Green Group
SQUADRON LEADERS: Hera Syndulla (Phoenix Leader), Arvel Crynyd (Green Leader)
APPEARANCES: R, VI
SEE ALSO: Admiral Ackbar; Lando Calrissian

Comlink helps pilots communicate during missions

A-WINGS ARE small, super-fast starfighters and A-wing pilots are some of the most talented fliers in the Rebel Alliance. These pilots play a pivotal role at the Battle of Endor when they destroy Vader's ship, the *Executor*.

Flak vest

Pressurized g-suit

Data cylinders

Rebel pilot Arvel Crynyd pilots his damaged A-wing into the bridge of the *Executor*.

Gear harness

A-WING starfighters started serving the Rebellion before the Battle of Yavin. Earlier versions of the craft were the mainstay vessels of Phoenix Squadron, a rebel cell operating in and around the Lothal sector in the Outer Rim Territories.

Capable Ships
Only the very best rebel pilots can fly the powerful A-wings. Originally designed as an escort ship, the A-wing's incredible speed and maneuverability make it a deadly strike craft. A-wings also use concealed sensors to gather information on Imperial ships.

B'OMARR MONK

MYSTERIOUS DISEMBODIED MONKS

DATA FILE

AFFILIATION: Jabba's court
MONASTERY LOCATIONS:
Tatooine; Teth
APPEARANCES: VI
SEE ALSO: Jabba the Hutt

THE B'OMARR MONKS are the original inhabitants of Jabba the Hutt's palace on Tatooine. When these mysterious monks reach the highest state of enlightenment, their living brains are surgically removed from their bodies and placed in special jars. These jars are carried around on mechanical legs.

Monk's Monastery

B'omarr monks still roam Jabba's palace. Jabba enjoys the gruesome sight of them! The oldest monks have four legs, while more recent ones have six.

B'OMARR MONKS

communicate telepathically. They go about their secret ways, ignoring the many bandits and smugglers who have inhabited their monastery over the centuries.

Brain support unit

Telepath response unit

Spider-like leg

The B'omarr monks built the monastery that Jabba the Hutt took as his palace on Tatooine.

Disembodied monk brain

Manipulator claw

BAIL ORGANA

VICEROY OF ALDERAAN

DATA FILE

AFFILIATION:
Republic/Rebel Alliance
HOMEWORLD: Alderaan
SPECIES: Human
HEIGHT: 1.91m (6ft 3in)
APPEARANCES: II, CW, III, R
SEE ALSO: Princess Leia;
Mon Mothma

Alderaanian cloak

Target blaster

ORGANA remains loyal to the Republic and the Jedi Order to the end. In Imperial times, it is Bail who responds to the threat of the Death Star by sending his adopted daughter, Leia, on a mission to locate Obi-Wan Kenobi in order to recruit him to the Rebel Alliance.

Action boots

After Order 66, Bail assists any survivors that he can.

Bail and his wife, Breha, adopt Leia Amidala Skywalker.

BAIL ORGANA is the Senator for Alderaan. He watches, horrified, as the Galactic Republic becomes a dictatorship under Palpatine. Bail, with Mon Mothma, is one of the founders of the Rebellion against Emperor Palpatine.

Forearm plate

Alderaanian belt

Narrow Escape

Bail is the first civilian to arrive at the Jedi Temple after the massacres carried out by Anakin and his legion of clone troopers. Bail narrowly escapes the Temple with his own life.

BALA-TIK

GUAVIAN FRONTMAN

AN AGENT FOR the Guavian Death Gang, Bala-Tik's patience with Han Solo has been worn out by one too many excuses for failed payments. Bala-Tik brings a group of security soldiers with him to collect what is due from Han.

Armored lining in coat

Gorraslug-leather coat

Percussive cannon

Bala-Tik and the rest of the Guavians carry black market technology, such as experimental percussive cannons.

Hunting Solo

Bala-Tik's bosses have ordered him to make an example of Solo. He forges an unlikely alliance with the Kanjiklub gang as they are also owed tens of thousands of credits by Han. After hunting Solo down, Bala-Tik discovers a droid in Solo's possession that the First Order is searching for, and sees an irresistible opportunity to profit.

BANTHA

TATOOINIAN BEASTS OF BURDEN

DATA FILE

HABITAT: Desert
HEIGHT: 2.5m (8ft 2in)
DIET: Herbivorous
LIFESPAN: 80-100 years
APPEARANCES: I, II, CW, IV, VI
SEE ALSO: Tusken Raider

FOR FARMERS AND SETTLERS on Tatooine, a Tusken Raider riding a bantha is a dreaded sight. Tusken Raiders form close bonds with these huge beasts, and use them to carry riders and transport belongings. They even make banthas members of their clans.

Tusken Rider

Tusken Raiders ride banthas in single file to hide their numbers. Tuskens are bonded with a single bantha from a young age.

Spiral horn

Sack for food and supplies

BOTH MALE and female banthas have spiral horns, which grow at a rate of a knob a year. Banthas can go without food or water for several weeks, making them suited to life in harsh environments like Tatooine.

Herds of banthas wander the dunes and wastes, led by a dominant female.

Three-toed hoof

BARRISS OFFEE

MIRIALAN PADAWAN AND TRAITOR

DATA FILE

AFFILIATION: Jedi
HOMEWORLD: Mirial
SPECIES: Mirialan
HEIGHT: 1.66m (5ft 5in)
APPEARANCES: II, CW
SEE ALSO: Luminara Unduli;
Shaak Ti

PADAWAN BARRISS OFFEE is a thoughtful, daring, and studious Jedi. She is the Padawan learner of Master Luminara Unduli. Barriss is a loyal apprentice who adheres closely to the Jedi Code until the trials of the Clone Wars change her point of view.

Mirialan tattoos

Two-handed grip for control

Belt contains secret compartment

BARRISS OFFEE came to view the Jedi role in the Clone Wars as a betrayal of the Order's ideals. She lashes out against her own kind in a rash and violent manner, orchestrating a bombing of the Jedi Temple and framing a fellow Padawan for the crime. Barriss is discovered and imprisoned.

Offee practiced a style of lightsaber fighting known as Soresu.

Hooded robe

Powerful Team

Offee specialized in tandem fighting and used the Force to keep her actions perfectly in sync with her partner Unduli. The team of Unduli and Offee was more powerful than the sum of its parts.

BATTLE DROID

MECHANICAL DROID SOLDIERS

DATA FILE

AFFILIATION: Separatists
TYPE: B1 battle droid
MANUFACTURER: Baktoid Armor Workshop
HEIGHT: 1.91m (6ft 3in)
APPEARANCES: I, II, CW, III
SEE ALSO: Droideka; super battle droid

Simple vocoder

Battle droids are first deployed against the peaceful people of Naboo.

E-5 blaster rifle

Arm extension piston

BATTLE DROIDS are the ground troops of the Separatist army: fearless, emotionless, and ready to do their masters' bidding. Battle droids are designed to resemble their Geonosian creators.

BATTLE DROIDS are intended to win by strength of numbers rather than by individual ability. The droids are mass-produced and unable to think independently. A computer on board a Trade Federation ship feeds them all their mission commands.

Folding knee joint

Limbs resemble humanoid skeletons

STAPs

Battle droid scouts and snipers are swept through the air on armed Single Trooper Aerial Platforms, or STAPs. These repulsorlift vehicles can thread through dense forests that would be inaccessible to larger vehicles.

Pilot droids operate the vast Separatist fleets.

BAZINE NETAL

DEEP COVER SPY

DATA FILE

AFFILIATION: Highest bidder
HOMEWORLD: Chaaktil
SPECIES: Human
HEIGHT: 1.7m (5ft 7in)
APPEARANCES: VII
SEE ALSO: Grummgar;
Maz Kanata; Kanjiklub gang

AN ALLURING and dangerous woman of intrigue lurking in the shadows of Maz Kanata's castle, Bazine Netal is a master of cloak and dagger. She uses her skills of deception to coax secrets from the unwitting and the unwilling.

Custom-styled light-absorbing shroud

Baffleweave patterning

Bazine sits with Grummgar, a big game hunter who frequents Maz Kanata's castle. From this vantage point, Bazine can see all that transpires in the castle.

BAZINE LEARNED

the fundamentals of self-defense living in the dangerous streets of Chaako City, the biggest urban center on Chaaktil. Bazine trained under Delphi Kloda, a grizzled former pirate Kanjiklubber who was the closest thing to a father she ever knew. As a result, Bazine is an expert unarmed combatant.

Vanishing Act

Though Bazine prefers to rely on her own skills rather than technology, she nonetheless keeps sophisticated tools in her arsenal. The complex patterns on her dress are lined with sensor-jamming baffleweave, an electronically-impregnated fabric that causes her to disappear from scanner readings.

BB-8

LOYAL ASTROMECH DROID

DATA FILE

AFFILIATION: Resistance
TYPE: Astromech droid
MANUFACTURER: Unknown
HEIGHT: 0.67m (2ft 2in)
APPEARANCES: VII
SEE ALSO: Rey; Poe
Dameron; Finn; R2-D2

High frequency
receiver antenna

Primary
photoreceptor

Swappable
tool bay

AN INTENSELY LOYAL astromech, BB-8 bravely rolls into danger when carrying out its assignments. The droid becomes the subject of an intense First Order search when it carries information that could lead to Luke Skywalker.

AS AN ASTROMECH droid, BB-8's small, spherical body is designed to fit into the droid socket of an X-wing starfighter. From that position BB-8 can manage the essential systems of the vessel, make repairs, and plot courses through space.

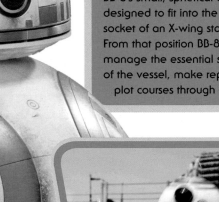

BB-8 speaks in beeps and whirs, and can project holograms.

Ball Droid

A complex drive system and wireless telemetry keep BB-8 on the move, tumbling its body forward while keeping its head upright. When situations require greater stability, BB-8 can deploy cables from compressed launchers that then anchor the droid in place, or allow it to reel itself into hard-to-reach places.

BERU LARS

LUKE SKYWALKER'S GUARDIAN

DATA FILE

AFFILIATION: None
HOMEWORLD: Tatooine
SPECIES: Human
HEIGHT: 1.65m (5ft 5in)
APPEARANCES: II, III, IV
SEE ALSO: Owen Lars;
Luke Skywalker

Simple hairstyle

BERU LARS'S family has been made up of moisture farmers for three generations. At the end of the Clone Wars, Obi-Wan Kenobi asks Beru and her husband, Owen, to raise Luke Skywalker, while he lives nearby to watch over the boy.

Desert tunic

Beru meets Anakin Skywalker when he investigates his mother's kidnapping.

Rough clothing made in Anchorhead

BERU LARS is hard-working and self-reliant. She is well equipped to deal with most of the dangers encountered in the Tatooine desert. However, nothing can prepare Beru for the group of Imperial stormtroopers that come in search of the two renegade droids carrying stolen Death Star plans.

Protector

As Luke becomes a young adult, Beru understands his desire to leave home and join the Imperial Academy. But she also knows the truth about Luke's father, and respects Owen's desire to protect Luke from following in Anakin's footsteps.

Desert boots

BIB FORTUNA

JABBA'S TWI'LEK MAJOR-DOMO

THE SINISTER BIB FORTUNA oversees the day-to-day affairs of Jabba the Hutt's desert palace and his estate in Mos Eisley. Before working with Jabba, Bib Fortuna became rich as a slave trader of his own people, the Twi'leks.

Lekku (head-tails; one of two)

Fortuna hovers near Jabba's ear, whispering advice. Secretly, he plots to kill Jabba!

Silver bracelet

Traditional Ryloth robe

Tricked

Bib Fortuna has been Jabba's major-domo (head of staff) for many decades. When two droids arrive unexpectedly to bargain for Han Solo's life, Fortuna unwittingly kickstarts a chain of events that leads to the downfall of the notorious Hutt gangster.

BIB FORTUNA is a powerful and dreaded individual in Jabba's entourage. Whether you are a friend or a foe, Fortuna will use underhand means against you in order to maintain his control within the organization.

Soft-soled shoes for silent creeping

BOBA FETT

THE BEST BOUNTY HUNTER IN THE GALAXY

DATA FILE

AFFILIATION: Bounty hunter
HOMEWORLD: Kamino
SPECIES: Human clone
HEIGHT: 1.83m (6ft)
APPEARANCES: II, CW, IV, V, VI
SEE ALSO: Jango Fett;
Darth Vader; Han Solo;
Jabba the Hutt

COOL AND CALCULATING, Boba Fett is a legendary bounty hunter. He is paid to track down and, often, kill targeted individuals. Over the years, Fett has developed a code of honor, and only accepts missions which meet this harsh sense of justice.

Multifunction helmet

EE-3 blaster rifle

Reinforced flight suit

Utility belt

On his first mission for Vader, Boba unwittingly reveals that Vader's son is alive by discovering that a Skywalker destroyed the Death Star.

BOBA FETT'S talent and skill, combined with an arsenal of exotic weapons, has brought in many "impossible" bounties. He is notorious for completely disintegrating those whom he has been hired to track down.

Like Father, Like Son

Boba Fett is an exact genetic clone of Jango Fett, who brings Boba up as a son. Boba witnesses Jango's death at the Battle of Geonosis and swears revenge against the Jedi who killed him. In time, he inherits Jango Fett's Mandalorian battle armor and his ship, *Slave I*.

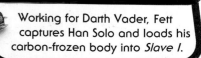

Working for Darth Vader, Fett captures Han Solo and loads his carbon-frozen body into *Slave I*.

BOBBAJO

CRITTERMONGER AND STORYTELLER

DATA FILE

AFFILIATION: None
HOMEWORLD: Jakku
SPECIES: Nu-Cosian
HEIGHT: 1.14m (3ft 9in)
APPEARANCES: VII
SEE ALSO: Teedo; Rey; Unkar Plutt

SHUFFLING HIS rare animal merchandise to various marketplaces and trading posts is Bobbajo, known to many simply as the Crittermonger. He is also known as the Storyteller, for his habit of spinning long and unlikely yarns.

Sneep

Head wrapping

Long, flexible neck

THE CREAKY-JOINTED Nu-Cosian

has an unflappable, kind personality that has a calming effect on the jittery creatures he keeps in his cages. It also lends a magical quality to his storytelling, as his gentle nature attracts many listeners.

Old Wanderer

Bobbajo has been a fixture on Jakku and nearby worlds for decades. To ensure he always has exotic merchandise, he braves the most treacherous terrain, including the crumbling cliffs of Carbon Ridge. He trudges through the shifting landscape as if following his own peculiar rhythm, ignoring the many dangers that surround him.

BOGA

OBI-WAN KENOBI'S MOUNT ON UTAPAU

DATA FILE

HOMEWORLD: Utapau
LENGTH: 15m (49ft)
DIET: Herbivorous
HABITAT: Arid scrubland, Utapaun sinkholes
APPEARANCES: III
SEE ALSO: Utai

BOGA IS A DOMESTICATED varactyl. On Utapau, Obi-Wan Kenobi rides Boga across the planet's hazardous sinkholes and sheer cliff faces in search of General Grievous. Boga is well-trained and highly responsive to the Jedi's command.

Boga and Kenobi plunge down a sinkhole after turncoat clones unleash a hail of blaster fire.

Crest present in both male and female

Spines for defense

VARACTYLS have powerful limbs and clawed feet, which makes them fast runners and excellent climbers. On Utapau, they are coralled by wranglers and used as transports.

Five-clawed feet provide excellent purchase

Swift Boga

Boga, with Obi-Wan Kenobi in the saddle, keeps pace with General Grievous on his Wheel Bike. After many twists and turns, Obi-Wan, with Boga's help, confronts and destroys the General.

BOSS NASS

DATA FILE

AFFILIATION: Gungan Rep Council, Gungan Grand Army
HOMEWORLD: Naboo
SPECIES: Gungan
HEIGHT: 2.06m (6ft 9in)
APPEARANCES: I, III
SEE ALSO: Padmé Amidala; Jar Jar Binks

Crown of rulership

Epaulets of military authority

Four-fingered hand

The Gungan High Council has the power to summon the Gungan Grand Army.

BOSS NASS is the stern, old-fashioned ruler of Otoh Gunga, the largest of the Gungan underwater cities on Naboo. He speaks Galactic Basic (the most widely used language in the galaxy) with a strong accent.

BOSS NASS

sits on the Gungan High Council. He is a fair but stubborn ruler. He particularly resents the Naboo's belief that the Gungans are primitive simply because Gungans prefer to use traditional crafts and technologies.

Long coat with golden clasp

For Jar Jar's help during the Naboo blockade, Nass reverses his banishment from Otoh Gunga.

Teamwork

When his planet is faced with invasion, Boss Nass puts aside his prejudice against the Naboo. He receives Queen Amidala when she humbly asks him for help. Boss Nass realizes that his people must work together with the Naboo or die, and a new friendship is forged between the two cultures.

BOSSK

TRANDOSHAN BOUNTY HUNTER

Eyes can see
in infrared
range

THE TOUGH AND RESILIENT Bossk is a reptilian Trandoshan bounty hunter. He used to track runaway slaves. Now he claims bounties for the Empire, and is incredibly successful at capturing his prey.

Sling for
grenade launcher

Flak vest

Relby v-10 micro
grenade launcher

BOSSK began his career doing a form of bounty hunting that few other species would risk: hunting Wookiees. Later, he hunts other species. During the Clone Wars, Bossk teams up with Aurra Sing, young Boba Fett, and a Klatooinian bounty hunter named Castas.

Lost fingers, skin, and
even limbs can regrow
until adulthood

Bossk and other bounty hunters frequently visit Jabba the Hutt, seeking their next job.

Tough Trandoshan

Fond of skinning his captives when possible, Bossk is as vile and mean as bounty hunters get. He is one of the six bounty hunters Darth Vader enlists to track down and capture the *Millennium Falcon*.

33

BOUSHH

PRINCESS LEIA IN DISGUISE

DATA FILE

AFFILIATION: Bounty hunter
HOMEWORLD: Uba IV
SPECIES Ubese
HEIGHT: 1.5m (4ft 11in)
APPEARANCES: VI
SEE ALSO: Princess Leia;
Chewbacca;
Jabba the Hutt

Speech scrambler

Glove spikes

Projectile detonator

Ammo pouch

Shata leather pants

Traditional Ubese boots

Leia, in disguise as Boushh, prepares to release Han Solo from frozen captivity.

BOUSHH'S survival clothing fits Leia perfectly. The real Boushh worked for many paymasters, but his downfall came when he accepted work from—and then tried to blackmail—the Black Sun crime syndicate.

THE GALAXY contains many bizarre creatures acting as bounty hunters (or claiming to be). Princess Leia adopts a convincing identity as an Ubese tracker, Boushh, to gain entry to Jabba's palace. Only Jabba suspects her identity is false.

Jabba's suspicions prove correct as he catches Leia unmasked with Han.

Boushh's Bounty

At Jabba's palace, Chewbacca pretends to be Boushh's captive, and Boushh demands a high price for the captured Wookiee. When Jabba disagrees over the amount of credits, Boushh pulls out a thermal detonator.

BUZZ DROID

SEPARATIST SABOTAGE DROIDS

DATA FILE

AFFILIATION: Separatists
TYPE: Pistoeka sabotage droid
MANUFACTURER: Colicoid Creation Nest
WIDTH: 25cm (10in)
APPEARANCES: CW, III
SEE ALSO: Obi-Wan Kenobi; R2-D2

BUZZ DROIDS are small droids used by the Separatist armies. Swarms of buzz droids attack enemy ships, dodging their way through defenses with their maneuvering thrusters. They use their manipulator arms and cutting tools to inflict as much damage as possible.

Under Attack

In the Battle of Coruscant, buzz droids attack Obi-Wan's starfighter and destroy his astromech droid, R4-P17.

Feisty R2-D2 targets a buzz droid's weak point: its primary photoreceptor eye.

SEPARATIST droid tri-fighters and vulture droid starfighters fire jet-powered discord missiles at enemy targets. Each discord missile contains up to seven buzz droids, enclosed in spherical casings that split open to reveal the droid inside.

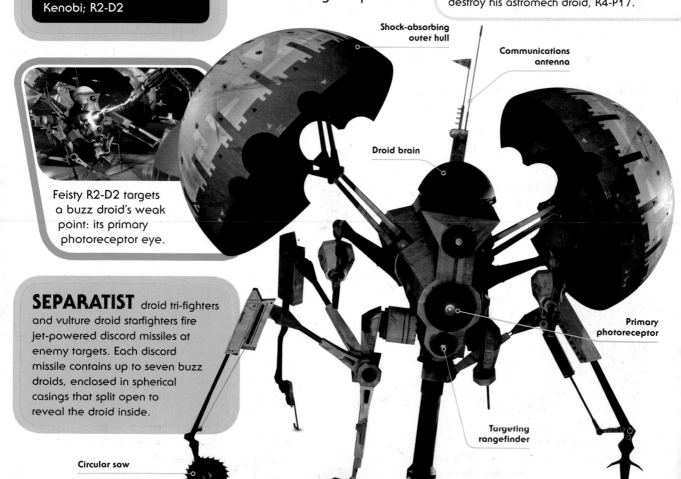

Shock-absorbing outer hull

Communications antenna

Droid brain

Primary photoreceptor

Targeting rangefinder

Circular saw

C-3PO

GOLDEN PROTOCOL DROID

DATA FILE

Vocabulator

AFFILIATION: Republic/
Rebel Alliance/Resistance
TYPE: Protocol droid
MANUFACTURER: Cybot
Galactica
HEIGHT: 1.67m (5ft 6in)
APPEARANCES: I, II, CW, III,
R, IV, V, VI, VII
SEE ALSO: R2-D2;
Anakin Skywalker;
Luke Skywalker

C-3PO IS PROGRAMMED
to assist in matters of etiquette
and translation. Thrown into
a world of adventure, he is
often overwhelmed by the
action around him. But he
forms a capable team
when partnered with
the resourceful R2-D2.

Primary power
coupling outlet

Replacement arm
from another droid

Anakin Skywalker built
the working skeleton of
C-3PO from scrap parts.

Reinforced knee joint

C-3PO first works for Anakin
Skywalker and his mother, Shmi. Anakin
then gives C-3PO to Senator Padmé
Amidala as a wedding gift. After
Padmé's death, C-3PO is assigned to
Bail Organa, until Darth Vader captures
the *Tantive IV*. C-3PO escapes to
Tatooine and is sold to Luke Skywalker.

Golden God

Despite his fear of excitement, C-3PO has
led an adventurous life, often losing limbs
or bits of circuitry along the way (though
he is easily repaired). On Endor, a tribe
of Ewoks worships C-3PO as a "golden
god," which leads the Ewoks to support
the rebels and play a decisive role in
defeating the Empire.

CAPTAIN ANTILLES

CAPTAIN OF THE *TANTIVE IV*

DATA FILE

AFFILIATION: Republic/Rebel Alliance
HOMEWORLD: Alderaan
SPECIES: Human
HEIGHT: 1.88m (6ft 2in)
APPEARANCES: III, IV
SEE ALSO: Bail Organa; Princess Leia

CAPTAIN RAYMUS ANTILLES is commander of Bail Organa's fleet of diplomatic cruisers. Under the Empire, Antilles becomes a rebel and serves as captain of the *Tantive IV* under Organa's adopted daughter, Leia Organa.

Cape of Alderaanian nobility

Wrist guard

CAPTAIN ANTILLES is a highly capable pilot. He has taken part in many daring missions for the rebels, and has had notable success breaking through Imperial blockades.

Target blaster

The Alderaan royal family owns the diplomatic cruiser *Tantive IV*.

Flight boots

Stranglehold

In the battle over Tatooine, Darth Vader boards the *Tantive IV* and demands that Antilles surrenders the stolen Death Star plans. When he refuses, Vader destroys him.

CAPTAIN ITHANO

CRIMSON CORSAIR

DATA FILE

AFFILIATION: Pirate
HOMEWORLD: Unknown
SPECIES: Delphidian
HEIGHT: 1.93m (6ft 4in)
APPEARANCES: VII
SEE ALSO: Finn;
Maz Kanata

THE ERA OF LAWLESSNESS that follows the Galactic Civil War leads to the rise of the colorful pirate, Sidon Ithano. Ithano uses many flashy aliases, and tales of his exploits continue to grow.

Captured Kanjiklub rifle

Pirate Crew

Ithano pilots the *Meson Martinet*, and his pirate crew (which includes his one-legged First Mate Quiggold) runs a smooth ship. Finn very nearly joins Ithano's crew at Maz's castle, when he tries to find a new life after deserting from the First Order.

Ithano's polished Kaleesh war helmet conceals his Delphidian features.

Armorweave lined cape

ITHANO IS
extremely vain, and relishes tales of his deeds as the "Blood Buccaneer," the "Crimson Corsair," or the "Red Raider." His legend is so long ago the hard work of him; as many frightened vessels surrender without putting up a fight.

CAPTAIN NEEDA

COMMANDER OF THE *AVENGER*

DATA FILE

AFFILIATION: Empire
HOMEWORLD: Coruscant
SPECIES: Human
HEIGHT: 1.75m (5ft 9in)
APPEARANCES: V
SEE ALSO: Darth Vader;
Admiral Ozzel

CAPTAIN NEEDA IS COMMANDER of the Imperial Star Destroyer *Avenger*, which takes part in the search for the rebels' hidden bases. Needa follows the *Falcon* into an asteroid field and back out, but then loses the ship completely.

Standard-issue
officer's gloves

Imperial officer's tunic

Belt buckle with
data storage

LORTH NEEDA is a dependable and ruthless officer who served the Galactic Republic in the Clone Wars during the Battle of Coruscant, when General Grievous "kidnapped" Chancellor Palpatine. Now an Imperial officer, Needa fails to live up to Vader's exacting standards.

Needa fails to see that the *Falcon* "disappeared" by clinging to the side of his Star Destroyer.

No Mercy

When Needa loses sight of the *Falcon*, he apologizes to Vader, accepting full responsibility. Vader accepts Needa's apology—then Force-chokes him.

CAPTAIN PANAKA

NABOO HEAD OF SECURITY

DATA FILE

AFFILIATION: Royal Naboo Security Forces
HOMEWORLD: Naboo
SPECIES: Human
HEIGHT: 1.83m (6ft)
APPEARANCES: 1
SEE ALSO: Padmé Amidala

AS HEAD OF SECURITY for Queen Amidala on Naboo, Captain Panaka oversees every branch of the volunteer Royal Naboo Security Forces. During the invasion of Naboo, Panaka sees the dangerous state of affairs in the galaxy and argues for stronger security measures.

Leather jerkin

Utility belt

CAPTAIN PANAKA

gained combat experience in a Republic Special Task Force, fighting against space pilots in the sector containing the Naboo system.

High officer headgear

Stripes on coat indicate rank

After Queen Amidala's abdication, Panaka serves Queen Jamillia.

Royal Responsibility

Panaka is responsible for Queen Amidala's safety, accompanying her during the escape from Naboo. When the Queen returns to Naboo to reclaim her throne, Panaka is by her side, offering cover fire during the infiltration of the Palace.

CAPTAIN PHASMA

STORMTROOPER COMMANDER

DATA FILE

AFFILIATION: First Order
HOMEWORLD: Unknown
SPECIES: Human
HEIGHT: 2m in armor
(6ft 6in)
APPEARANCES: VII
SEE ALSO: Kylo Ren;
General Hux; Finn;
First Order stormtrooper

CLAD IN DISTINCTIVE metallic armor, Captain Phasma commands the First Order's legions of stormtroopers. She sees it as her duty to ensure only the best soldiers serve the First Order.

Chromium-plated
F-11D blaster rifle

Crush gauntlets

Armorweave cape

When FN-2187, a stormtrooper under her command, abandons his duties and defects to the Resistance, Phasma takes it as a personal failing.

DESPITE HER RANK, Phasma prefers being in the thick of combat operations, witnessing battle firsthand and fighting alongside her troops. Her armor is coated in salvaged Nabba chromium that offers protection and emphasizes her authority.

Forged in Battle

Phasma believes that true soldiers are only made in combat. Though she recognizes the value of the complex simulations used in stormtrooper training, she thinks that success in simulations is no real guarantee of a soldier's bravery.

CAPTAIN TYPHO

SENATOR AMIDALA'S HEAD OF SECURITY

DATA FILE

AFFILIATION: Royal Naboo Security Forces
HOMEWORLD: Naboo
SPECIES: Human
HEIGHT: 1.85m (6ft 1in)
APPEARANCES: II, CW, III
SEE ALSO: Padmé Amidala; Captain Panaka

CAPTAIN TYPHO is well respected for his loyalty. His uncle, Captain Panaka, was head of security for Padmé Amidala when she was Queen of Naboo. Now Typho oversees security for Padmé in her role as Senator for Naboo.

Security uniform

Eye lost during battle of Naboo

Synthetic leather gauntlets

Naboo blaster

AT THE TIME of the Battle of Naboo, Typho was a Junior Palace Guard. Despite his young age, Typho played a brave part in the conflict, losing his eye in the line of duty. Captain Typho is given his Senatorial post because of his loyalty and his ties to Panaka.

Captain Typho is by Amidala's side on many missions throughout the Clone Wars.

A Dangerous World

Captain Typho accompanies Senator Amidala to Coruscant, where an assassination attempt kills seven in his command, including Padmé's handmaiden Cordé (disguised as Padmé). Typho soon realizes that even his strict security measures might not be enough in the new, dangerous world of the Clone Wars.

CHANCELLOR VALORUM

DATA FILE

AFFILIATION: Republic
HOMEWORLD: Coruscant
SPECIES: Human
HEIGHT: 1.7m (5ft 7in)
APPEARANCES: I, CW
SEE ALSO: Palpatine; Padmé Amidala; Mas Amedda

BEFORE PALPATINE becomes Supreme Chancellor, Finis Valorum holds the highest position in the Galactic Senate. He rules the Republic when Trade Federation warships blockade the peaceful planet of Naboo. Padmé Amidala blames Valorum personally.

Ornate overcloak

Blue band symbolic of Supreme Chancellor

When Valorum resigns, Senator Palpatine steps in, promising strength and effectiveness.

Veda cloth robe

VALORUM comes from a family of politicians. All his life, he has been preparing for the office of Supreme Chancellor. This is a man who enjoys the privileges of a head of state. However, this attitude does not endear him to ordinary voters.

Weak Leader

While Naboo suffers, the Senate debates its options but does not act. The Speaker, Mas Amedda (secretly working for Palpatine), knows that this indecision will make Valorum look weak and ineffective.

CHEWBACCA

WOOKIEE WARRIOR, PILOT, AND HERO

DATA FILE

AFFILIATION: Rebel Alliance/Resistance
HOMEWORLD: Kashyyyk
SPECIES: Wookiee
HEIGHT: 2.28m (7ft 6in)
APPEARANCES: CW, III, IV, V, VI, VII
SEE ALSO: Han Solo; Tarfful

Bowcaster

Water-shedding hair

Tool pouch

CHEWBACCA is a Wookiee mechanic and pilot. During the Clone Wars, he fights to defend his planet. In the time of the Empire, he is first mate and loyal friend to Han Solo aboard the *Millennium Falcon*.

CHEWIE SERVES

as Han Solo's fiercely loyal copilot and trusty fellow adventurer. He enjoys the thrilling action that Solo gets them into, but sometimes tries to act as a check on his partner's willfulness.

Wookiee Mechanic

The great Wookiee uses his mechanical abilities to keep Solo's starship flying. Later, he will employ these skills to completely reconstruct C-3PO after the poor droid is blasted apart on Cloud City.

Thirty years after the Rebellion, Han and Chewie are still side by side.

CHIEF CHIRPA

DATA FILE

AFFILIATION: Bright Tree Village
HOMEWORLD: Forest moon of Endor
SPECIES: Ewok
HEIGHT: 1m (3ft 3in)
APPEARANCES: VI
SEE ALSO: Logray; Teebo

WISE CHIEF CHIRPA has led the Bright Tree tribe on the forest moon of Endor for 42 seasons. When his Ewok tribe captures a Rebel Alliance strike force, Chirpa is only stopped from sacrificing them by C-3PO, whom the superstitious Ewoks believe is a "golden god."

Hood

Acute sense of smell

Chief's medallion

Reptilian staff

CHIEF Chirpa leads his village with understanding, though he has become a bit forgetful in his old age. His authority commits the Ewoks to their dangerous fight against the Empire.

Hunting knife

The Bright Tree tribe lives in a village high up in the treetops.

New Recruits

After listening to C-3PO's account of the resistance to the Empire, Chirpa commits the Ewoks to the struggle. In the Battle of Endor, the Ewok warriors use all their cunning and fierceness to defeat the superior forces of the Imperial army.

CLIEGG LARS

DATA FILE

AFFILIATION: None
HOMEWORLD: Tatooine
SPECIES: Human
HEIGHT: 1.83m (6ft)
APPEARANCES: II
SEE ALSO: Shmi Skywalker;
Owen Lars; Beru Lars

WHEN TATOOINIAN moisture farmer Cliegg Lars goes looking for a farmhand in Mos Espa, he instead meets a slave and falls in love. The slave is Shmi Skywalker, Anakin Skywalker's mother. In order to marry Shmi, Cliegg buys her freedom from Watto, the flying junk dealer who owns her.

Gear harness

Weather-worn
work clothes

Cliegg loses a leg in his attempt to rescue Shmi from Tusken Raiders.

CLIEGG'S father was a Tatooinian farmer, but young Cliegg wanted to experience life on a bustling Core World. Here, he fell in love with and married Aika. But when Aika died, Cliegg returned to Tatooine to run the family farm.

Heartbroken

Cliegg loses Shmi when Tusken Raiders kidnap and kill her. After her death, Cliegg remains determined to live the life he has worked so hard to create. Sadly, he dies shortly afterward from a broken heart.

CLONE PILOT

SPECIALIST CLONE AIRMEN

Anti-glare
blast visor

Rebreather
unit

Air-supply hose

Flight data
records pouch

FROM THE START of the Clone Wars, clones were trained to fly LAAT gunships. As the war progresses, a new breed are trained to fly the hyperspace-capable ARC-170 and V-wing starfighters.

A pilot and copilot/forward gunner fly an ARC-170 fighter at the Battle of Coruscant.

IN THE BATTLE OF

Coruscant, most clone pilots wear Phase II pilot armor, with helmets fitted with anti-glare blast visors. V-wing pilots, however, wear fully enclosed helmets since these ships carry no on-board life-support systems.

Gunship Pilots

At the start of the Clone Wars, in the Battle of Geonosis, clone pilots fly LAAT/i and LAAT/c gunships. They wear Phase I battle armor, distinguished by yellow markings and specialized full-face helmets.

CLONE TROOPER (PHASE I)

FIRST GENERATION CLONE TROOPERS

DATA FILE

AFFILIATION: Republic
HOMEWORLD: Kamino
SPECIES: Human clone
HEIGHT: 1.83m (6ft)
APPEARANCES: II, CW
SEE ALSO: Clone trooper (Phase II); clone pilot; Jango Fett

Clone troopers are deployed from Republic assault ships, which also carry gunships.

DC-15 blaster

Breath filter

Utility belt

Thigh plate

THE FIRST CLONE troopers are designated Phase I because of their style of armor. Born and raised in Kaminoan cloning factories, they are trained for no other purpose than to fight, and feel virtually invincible.

PHASE I armor is loosely based on Jango Fett's Mandalorian shock trooper armor. It consists of 20 armor plates and is often referred to as the "body bucket" because it is heavy and uncomfortable.

First Strike

When the Separatist droid army makes its first all-out strike on Geonosis, the Senate has no choice but to send in an army of clone soldiers that it has neither amassed nor trained. Under the skillful command of the Jedi, the clones force a droid retreat.

High-traction soles

CLONE TROOPER (PHASE II)

SECOND GENERATION CLONE TROOPERS

DATA FILE

AFFILIATION: Republic/Empire
HOMEWORLD: Kamino
SPECIES: Human clone
HEIGHT: 1.83m (6ft)
APPEARANCES: CW, III
SEE ALSO: Clone trooper
(Phase I)

Clone troops form the galaxy's best military force.

Battle-damaged chest plastron

Spare blaster magazine

Standard DC-15 blaster has a folding stock

BY THE TIME of the Battle of Coruscant, clone troopers, with enhanced Phase II armor, are battle-dented and mud-smeared. Aging at twice the rate of normally birthed humans, only two-thirds of the original army of clone troopers are alive.

Knee plate

PHASE II armor is stronger, lighter, and more adaptable than Phase I armor, and has many specialist variations.

Superior Troopers

Clone troopers are equipped with far more advanced armor and air support than the Separatists, allowing them to easily cut through the battle droid ranks.

COLEMAN TREBOR

VURK JEDI MASTER

DATA FILE

AFFILIATION: Jedi
HOMEWORLD: Sembla
SPECIES: Vurk
HEIGHT: 2.13m (7ft)
APPEARANCES: II
SEE ALSO: Yarael Poof;
Count Dooku

Bony head
crest grows
through life

Thick
reptilian skin

Coleman Trebor joined the Jedi
High Council after the death of Jedi
Master Yarael Poof.

JEDI MASTER Coleman
Trebor is revered as
a skillful mediator,
bringing difficult disputes
to a harmonious end.
His skill with a lightsaber
is also impressive,
and he joins Windu's
taskforce to Geonosis.

Food and
energy capsules

Jedi cloak

Facing Dooku

On Geonosis, Coleman Trebor
seizes his opportunity and steps
up to Count Dooku, taking the
Separatist leader by surprise. But
bounty hunter Jango Fett quickly
fires his blaster at the noble Jedi,
who falls to his death.

COLEMAN TREBOR

is a Vurk from the oceanic world
of Sembla. His species is thought
to be primitive, but they are in
fact highly empathetic and
serene. Trebor's Force potential
was spotted early on, and he
joined the Jedi Order, the only
Vurk known to have done so.

COMMANDER BACARA

KI-ADI-MUNDI'S CLONE COMMANDER

DATA FILE

AFFILIATION:
Republic/Empire
HOMEWORLD: Kamino
SPECIES: Human clone
HEIGHT: 1.83m (6ft)
APPEARANCES: III
SEE ALSO: Ki-Adi-Mundi;
clone trooper (Phase II)

Blizzard
protection
side plates

Bacara and snow armor-clad
Galactic Marines fight on
planet Mygeeto.

DC-15
blaster rifle

CLONE COMMANDER

Bacara (also known as
CC-1138) received ARC training.
The ARC program turns ordinary
clones into leaders by developing
their individual thinking. Bacara
serves Jedi Master Ki-Adi-Mundi.

Utility belt

Kneecap
armor

Battle of Mygeeto

Commander Bacara fights alongside
Ki-Adi-Mundi in many battles. At the end
of the Clone Wars, the two warriors travel
to the snow-covered world of Mygeeto,
where Republic forces have been fighting
droids for two years. Bacara leads his
fellow marines through Mygeeto's cities.

BEFORE TAKING

part in ARC training, Bacara
was one of the few clones
who trained with an ex-
Journeyman Protector, lawmen
from the Mandalorian world of
Concord Dawn, rather than
with Fett's hand-picked bounty
hunter instructors. For some,
this explains Bacara's
reputation as a loner.

COMMANDER BLY

DATA FILE

AFFILIATION:
Republic/Empire
HOMEWORLD: Kamino
SPECIES: Human clone
HEIGHT: 1.83m (6ft)
APPEARANCES: CW, III
SEE ALSO: Aayla Secura;
clone trooper (Phase II)

Helmet contains
oxygen supply

After Order 66
turns him against
the Republic, Bly
serves the Empire.

Plastoid armor
pitted from
shrapnel strikes

COMMANDER BLY
is a clone of Jango
Fett. He was part of the
first wave of clone
commanders trained by
the Advanced Recon
Commando (ARC)
troopers. Bly's focus is
entirely on the success
of each mission.

Quick-release holster
for DC-17 repeater
hand blaster

Cold Commander

Clone Commander Bly and Jedi General
Aayla Secura are hunting down Separatist
leader Shu Mai on the exotic world of
Felucia when Bly receives Palpatine's Order
66. Without a moment's hesitation, the
clone soldier guns down the Jedi Knight
he had served with on so many missions.

CLONE COMMANDER

CC-5052, or Bly, has
worked closely with Jedi
General Aayla Secura, and
respects her dedication to
completing the mission.

COMMANDER CODY

OBI-WAN KENOBI'S CLONE COMMANDER

DATA FILE

AFFILIATION: Republic/Empire
HOMEWORLD: Kamino
SPECIES: Human clone
HEIGHT: 1.83m (6ft)
APPEARANCES: CW, III
SEE ALSO: Clone trooper (Phase II); Obi-Wan Kenobi

Breath filter

This variant of Phase II armor features one antenna

Cody's last loyal action: returning Kenobi's lost lightsaber to the Jedi.

DC-15 blaster rifle yields 300 shots on maximum power

CLONE UNIT 2224, known as Commander Cody, is often assigned to Jedi General Obi-Wan Kenobi. He is one of the original clones from Kamino. His extra training developed leadership ability.

Color denotes legion affiliation

CLONE COMMANDERS

like Cody use names in addition to numerical designations. The Jedi and progressive-thinking Republic officials initiated this practice in order to foster a growing fellowship. This is why CC-2224 came to be called Cody.

High-traction boots

Sidious in Charge

Cody fights loyally and bravely alongside General Kenobi on many missions in the Clone Wars, including on Lola Sayu and Utapau. They have established an easy-going camaraderie. Nevertheless, when Cody receives Palpatine's Order 66 to destroy the Jedi, he does so without giving his betrayal a second thought.

COMMANDER GREE

DATA FILE

AFFILIATION: Republic
HOMEWORLD: Kamino
SPECIES: Human clone
HEIGHT: 1.83m (6ft)
APPEARANCES: CW, III
SEE ALSO: Yoda;
Luminara Unduli

Polarized
T-visor

Camouflage
markings

Weapons and
ammunition belt

CLONE UNIT 1004

chose the name Gree to
express his interest in the
wide and varied alien
cultures found throughout
the galaxy. The Gree is a
little-known alien species.

Reinforced
tactical boots

Armor
plates are
often replaced

Ultimately loyal only to Palpatine,
Gree attempts to kill Yoda. But
Yoda strikes down the clone.

CLONE COMMANDER GREE

commands the 41st Elite Corps
in the Clone Wars. Led by Jedi
General Luminara Unduli, the 41st
specializes in long-term missions
on alien worlds. Gree uses his
knowledge of the customs of
alien species to help build
alliances with local populations.

Wookiee Defenders

Gree serves under Jedi Master Yoda at
the Battle of Kashyyyk. Gree's camouflage
armor provides cover in the green jungles
of the Wookiee planet. His battle-hardened
clone troopers are also equipped
for jungle warfare.

COMMANDER NEYO

STASS ALLIE'S CLONE COMMANDER

DATA FILE

AFFILIATION:
Republic/Empire
HOMEWORLD: Kamino
SPECIES: Human clone
HEIGHT: 1.83m (6ft)
APPEARANCES: CW, III
SEE ALSO: Stass
Allie; clone
trooper (Phase II)

Enhanced
breath filter

Built-in comlink

Regiment markings

CLONE COMMANDER NEYO
is assigned to the 91st
Reconnaissance Corps, which
often utilizes BARC speeders.
Neyo fights many battles
in the Outer Rim sieges
during the Clone Wars.

ARC
command sash

Equipment
pouch

Neyo serves with Jedi Stass
Allie in the siege of the
Separatist planet Saleucami.

NEYO, or unit 8826, is one
of the first 100 graduates from the
experimental clone commander
training program on Kamino. Bred
solely for fighting, Neyo developed
a disturbingly cold personality.

Clone Betrayal

After the Republic captures Saleucami,
Neyo stays on to destroy the last
pockets of resistance. During a speeder
patrol with Stass Allie, Neyo receives
Order 66 and turns his laser
cannons on the Jedi General.

CONSTABLE ZUVIO

NIIMA OUTPOST LAWMAN

DATA FILE

AFFILIATION: Niima Outpost
HOMEWORLD: Jakku
SPECIES: Kyuzo
HEIGHT: 1.6m (5ft 3in)
APPEARANCES: VII
SEE ALSO: Teedo;
Unkar Plutt

Wrapped face to
protect from sun

Salvaged
metal armor

Vibro-halberd

A TOUGH AND humorless law officer at Niima Outpost on Jakku, Constable Zuvio tries to keep the salvage operation running smoothly. He vigilantly cracks down on cheats, thieves, and troublemakers.

ZUVIO AND HIS fellow Kyuzo lawmen are mainly charged with protecting the landing paddock at Niima, making sure no would-be thieves touch any of the visiting starships that are so essential to Jakku's fragile economy.

Honor and Justice

Zuvio has a strong sense of justice, unusual on a frontier world. He cannot be bribed and trusts only his fellow Kyuzo to have a similar code of honor. Though Zuvio carries a concealed blaster pistol, he prefers to deal with lawbreakers using his powerful voice or by brandishing his halberd.

COUNT DOOKU

SEPARATIST LEADER AND SITH LORD

DATA FILE

AFFILIATION: Sith, Separatists
HOMEWORLD: Serenno
SPECIES: Human
HEIGHT: 1.93m (6ft 4in)
APPEARANCES: II, CW, III
SEE ALSO: Palpatine;
Anakin Skywalker

Cape is emblem of Count of Serenno

Caught between Anakin's blades, Dooku is unprepared for Sidious's treachery.

COUNT DOOKU was once a Jedi Master. But his independent spirit led him away from the Order and he became a Sith apprentice, named Darth Tyranus. As Dooku, he leads the Separatist movement, which seeks independence from the Republic.

Curved lightsaber

COUNT DOOKU

is a member of the nobility on his homeworld of Serenno, and one of the richest men in the galaxy. He uses his wealth and power to convince many star systems to join his Separatist movement.

During the first battle of Geonosis, Dooku fights Yoda—his former master.

Boots of rare rancor leather

Sith Skills

Count Dooku is a formidable opponent. He Is a master of ancient Form II lightsaber combat, characterized by graceful moves. He can also project deadly streams of Sith Force lightning from his fingertips.

CRAB DROID

SIX-LEGGED BATTLE DROIDS

KNOWN TO CLONE troopers as "Muckrackers," Separatist crab droids are deployed during the Clone Wars on marshy worlds such as Utapau. These heavily armored weapons are made in a range of sizes, from small spy drones to huge trailblazers. Crab droids can also push their way through muck to create paths for infantry.

Weak Spot

Crab droids prove to be a threat to the clone troopers during the Battle of Utapau. However, some brave troopers escape their targeting sensors and find their weak spots behind the forward armor.

During the Clone Wars, the Techno Union develops and produces crab droids.

CRAB DROIDS'

powerful legs allow them to scuttle at high speeds on uneven terrain and even up craggy surfaces. Their front pincers also serve as vacuums, slurping up and spewing out lake-bed mud.

Armorplast shielding

Duranium stabilizer can push through bedrock

Sensor bulb

Twin blasters

DARTH MAUL

SITH SURVIVOR

DATA FILE

AFFILIATION: Sith, Nightbrothers
HOMEWORLD: Dathomir
SPECIES: Zabrak
HEIGHT: 1.75m (5ft 9in)
APPEARANCES: I, CW
SEE ALSO: Qui-Gon Jinn; Obi-Wan Kenobi; Palpatine

Face markings

Field cloak

Maul meets with his Sith Master, Darth Sidious.

DARTH MAUL IS Darth Sidious's apprentice and one of the most dangerous and highly trained Sith in the history of the Order. His entire body is marked with patterns that show his heritage as a part of the warrior tribe known as the Nightbrothers of Dathomir.

Lightsaber blade is red due to nature of internal crystals

Heavy-action boots

Maul Versus Kenobi

Sent to capture Queen Amidala during the invasion of Naboo, Maul gives Jedi Master Qui-Gon Jinn and Obi-Wan Kenobi the rare opportunity to fight a trained Sith warrior. Jinn first duels with Maul on Tatooine. He faces Maul a second time on Naboo, this time with Kenobi. Kenobi thought he had destroyed the evil Sith, but Maul survived the devastating wound.

DARTH MAUL was believed dead by the Jedi, but his lust for vengeance kept him alive. Reanimated by Nightsister magicks, Maul returned during the Clone Wars to wreak havoc in the criminal underworld before being captured by Darth Sidious. Maul once again narrowly escaped death.

DARTH VADER

DARK LORD OF THE SITH

DATA FILE

AFFILIATION: Sith
HOMEWORLD: Tatooine
SPECIES: Human
HEIGHT: (armored) 2.02m
(6ft 7in)
APPEARANCES: III, R, IV,
V, VI
SEE ALSO: Palpatine;
Luke Skywalker

Darth Vader fights the battle that
will result in his encasement
in a life-support suit.

THE GRIM, FORBIDDING
figure of Darth Vader is
Emperor Palpatine's
Sith apprentice and a
much-feared military
commander. Vader's
knowledge of the
dark side of the Force
makes him unnerving
and dangerous.

Control function panel

AFTER VADER'S
...defeat at the hands of
Obi-Wan Kenobi on
Mustafar, Palpatine has
his apprentice encased
in black armor. Vader
is unable to survive
without the constant life-
support provided
by his black suit.

Sith blade

Outer cloak

Palpatine is pleased with his
apprentice's terrifying new form.

Father and Son

When Vader learns that Luke Skywalker is his son,
he harbors a desire to turn Luke to the dark side
and rule the galaxy with him. Yet Luke refuses to
lose sight of Vader's humanity under the armor.

DEATH STAR GUNNER

IMPERIAL WEAPONS OPERATORS

DATA FILE

AFFILIATION: Empire
SPECIES: Human
HEIGHT: 1.8m (5ft 11in)
APPEARANCES: IV, VI
SEE ALSO: AT-AT pilot;
AT-ST pilot; stormtrooper

Black durasteel gloves

Energy-shielded fabric

Gunners on platforms monitor the titanic energy levels of the Death Star's superlaser.

DEATH STAR GUNNERS control the terrible weapons of the Empire's capital ships, military bases, and Death Star battlestations. Their elite skills with weapons are used to handle powerful turbolasers and ion cannons.

THE IMPERIAL navy equips Death Star gunners with specialized helmets with slit-eye like visors, designed to protect their eyes from the bright flashes of light from turbolaser and superlaser fire. Many gunners find that the helmets restrict all-round vision.

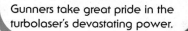

Gunners take great pride in the turbolaser's devastating power.

Positive gravity pressure boots

Turbolaser Gunners

The Empire's capital ships and its Death Star are bristling with turbolasers. A team of gunners man these heavy guns, which rotate on turrets. The gunners monitor crucial recharge timings and heat levels, while locking onto targets. A single blast can obliterate an enemy starfighter.

DEPA BILLABA

DATA FILE

AFFILIATION: Jedi
HOMEWORLD: Chalacta
SPECIES: Human
HEIGHT: 1.68m (5ft 6in)
APPEARANCES: I, II
SEE ALSO: Mace Windu;
Yoda; Qui-Gon Jinn

Chalactan marks
of illumination

Billaba offers an ordered
perspective to the wide-ranging
minds of her fellow Jedi.

JEDI MASTER Depa
Billaba serves on the
Jedi High Council
where she is known
to be a wise and
spiritual voice. She
serves as a Jedi
General during the
Clone Wars.

Jedi robes cover
practical fighting tunic

Lightsaber
worn on utility
belt under robes

Billaba usually
employs Form III in
close quarters fighting

BILLABA'S FORCES

suffered a devastating loss
against General Grievous at
Haruun Kal. The battle's physical
and psychological toll caused
some among the Jedi to wonder
if she would ever recover. Once
Billaba overcame her wounds,
she took a Padawan named
Caleb Dume. During Order
66, she sacrificed herself on
Kaller to ensure his survival.

Jedi Fellowship

Jedi Master Mace Windu rescued
Billaba from the space pirates who
destroyed her parents. Eventually,
Windu took Billaba as his
Padawan. Over the years, they
have developed a close bond.

DEWBACK

DATA FILE

HOMEWORLD: Tatooine
HEIGHT: 1.8m (5ft 11in)
DIET: Omnivorous
HABITAT: Desert
APPEARANCES: I, CW, VI
SEE ALSO: Sandtrooper

LARGE DEWBACK lizards live on the desert planet Tatooine. Locals use them for carrying heavy loads and as transport. During the time of the Empire, Imperial sandtroopers ride dewbacks on Tatooine in preference to their mechanical vehicles, which are more easily harmed by sand and heat.

Search Patrol

A squad of sandtroopers search the desert for signs of the droids who escaped from Princess Leia's ship with stolen Death Star plans. Imperial sandtroopers often ride dewbacks when carrying out security and military patrols.

C-3PO and R2-D2 look on nervously while a sandtrooper dismounts to interrogate a local.

DEWBACKS ARE reclusive by nature and can be found roaming the desert in small packs of two to five. During the day, they forage for food and moisture. When the temperature drops at night, they huddle together to keep warm.

Body adapted for living in desert

Saddle harnessed to dewback

Claws

Powerful, load-bearing haunches

DEXTER JETTSTER

BESALISK COOK AND INFORMANT

DATA FILE

AFFILIATION: None
HOMEWORLD: Ojom
SPECIES: Besalisk
HEIGHT: 1.9m (6ft 3in)
APPEARANCES: II
SEE ALSO: Obi-Wan Kenobi

Male Besalisk crest

Powerful arm

Dexterous fingers

Dexter is chief cook and bottle washer in his diner in an unfashionable part of Coruscant.

THE FOUR-ARMED
Besalisk named Dexter Jettster runs a diner on Coruscant. Dexter is an individual with diverse connections. This is why Obi-Wan Kenobi seeks him out when he needs information on a mysterious toxic saberdart that has killed assassin Zam Wesell.

THE GRUFF
but good-hearted Dexter Jettster spent many years manning oil rigs across the galaxy, tending bar, brawling, and running weapons on the side. On Coruscant, he has made a fresh start with his diner.

Informant
Beneath his sloppy exterior, Dexter has a keen sense of observation and a retentive memory. He can serve up vital information, even to the likes of a Jedi Knight such as Obi-Wan Kenobi.

DOCTOR EVAZAN

MURDEROUS CRIMINAL

DATA FILE

AFFILIATION: Smuggler
HOMEWORLD: Alsakan
SPECIES: Human
HEIGHT: 1.77m (5ft 10in)
APPEARANCES: IV
SEE ALSO: Ponda Baba

Facial scarring

Evazan and Ponda Baba pull blasters: Bartender Wuher ducks, but Kenobi stands his ground.

Weapons belt

CARRYING MULTIPLE death sentences, the murderous Doctor Evazan is notorious for rearranging body parts on living creatures. Evazan and his partner, Ponda Baba, also enjoy brawling and gunning down defenseless beings.

Holster

EVAZAN was once a promising surgeon. However, during his training he was corrupted by madness. He now practices "creative surgery" (without the assistance of droids) on hundreds of victims, leaving them hideously scarred.

Criminal Thug

Evazan is a smuggler and murderer with many enemies across the galaxy. A bounty hunter once tried to destroy Evazan, scarring his face. An Aqualish trouble-maker named Ponda Baba saved him and became his partner in crime.

DOCTOR KALONIA

RESISTANCE MEDICAL OFFICER

DATA FILE

AFFILIATION: Resistance
HOMEWORLD: Unknown
SPECIES: Human
HEIGHT: 1.73m (5ft 8in)
APPEARANCES: VII
SEE ALSO: Chewbacca;
Admiral Statura

DOCTOR KALONIA'S sympathetic bedside manner and good humor are often just what is needed to mend the spirits of wounded Resistance personnel. She is a skilled doctor and surgeon.

Military rank badge

Medical services armband

Resistance tunic

BASED AT THE Resistance headquarters on D'Qar, Doctor Kalonia makes do with an understaffed medical center. Prior to open conflict with the First Order, Kalonia's main duties involve dealing with the illnesses and exposure that the troops suffer in the exotic climate of the lush planet.

Comfortable boots for long hours spent standing

Medical Chief

Kalonia holds the military rank of major, though she can command greater authority over medical matters, relieving higher-ranking officers of duty if she feels it is necessary. She is also a skilled linguist—her fluency in the Wookiee language, Shyriiwook, helps soothe a nervous Chewbacca after he is wounded.

DROIDEKA

DESTROYER DROIDS

DATA FILE

AFFILIATION: Separatists
TYPE: Battle droid
MANUFACTURER: Colicoids
HEIGHT: 1.83m (6ft)
APPEARANCES: I, II, CW, III
SEE ALSO: Battle droid; super battle droid

DROIDEKAS ARE HEAVY DUTY destroying machines that back up battle droids in the face of determined opposition. They uncoil in a matter of seconds from wheel form into standing position, ready to attack. They also carry their own deflector shield generators to protect from enemy fire.

Fearsome Droids

Covered with heavy alloy or armor plate, droidekas cut down soldiers by the dozen with ease. Their deflector shield generators can completely repel pistol fire and weaken high-energy bolts.

Sensor head

Twin blaster

A SPECIES of insectoid Colicoids on the planet Colla IV created the design of the droideka in their own image. Colicoids are known for their completely unfeeling and murderous ways. The Trade Federation initially paid the Colicoids in exotic meats for shipments of the droids.

Moving leg

Mini-reactor bulb

For optimum travel speed, droidekas retract into the shape of a wheel.

DROOPY McCOOL

HORN PLAYER IN THE MAX REBO BAND

DATA FILE

AFFILIATION: Jabba's court
HOMEWORLD: Kirdo III
SPECIES: Kitonak
HEIGHT: 1.6m (5ft 3in)
APPEARANCES: VI
SEE ALSO: Max Rebo;
Jabba the Hutt

Tiny eyes
hidden by
folds of skin

After Jabba's death, McCool
disappears into the desert.

Tough,
leathery skin

Chidinkalu flute

Body releases a
vanilla-like smell

DROOPY McCOOL
is stage name of the
lead flute player in
the Max Rebo Band,
Jabba's house band.
A far-out quasi-mystic
Kitonak, Droopy's
real name is a series
of flute-like whistles,
unpronounceable by
any other species.

McCOOL is lonely
for the company of his
own kind and claims to
have heard the faint
tones of other Kitonaks
somewhere out in the
Tatooine dunes.

Jamming

Laidback Droopy is largely oblivious
to what is going on around him. He
hardly recognizes the stage name
that Max Rebo gave him—Droopy
just plays the tunes.

DWARF SPIDER DROID

FOUR-LEGGED BATTLE DROIDS

DATA FILE

AFFILIATION: Separatists
TYPE: DSD1 dwarf spider droids
MANUFACTURER: Baktoid Armor Workshop
HEIGHT: 1.98m (6ft 6in)
APPEARANCES: II, CW, III
SEE ALSO: Battle droid; homing spider droid

COMMERCE GUILD DWARF spider droids are more rugged than battle droids. Their four striding legs are designed for roadless terrain on rocky mining worlds. They are armed with head-mounted blaster cannons that are effective against infantry troops, and they can also easily destroy small vehicles.

Hunters

Dwarf spider droids are first used for warfare at the Battle of Geonosis. Until this time, the Commerce Guild used the droids to scuttle down narrow mine shafts to enforce tribute payments.

Photoreceptors see in infrared

Primary laser cannon

Devastating firepower is this droid's strength, but it is vulnerable from behind.

Armored body core

Clawed feet can climb up cliffs

DWARF SPIDER DROIDS

speak a form of binary droid language, and sometimes express frustration. If threatened on the battlefield, these dangerous droids can trigger a self-destruct mechanism.

EETH KOTH

JEDI HIGH COUNCIL MEMBER

Vestigial horns

JEDI MASTER AND JEDI High Council member Eeth Koth is an Iridonian Zabrak. This horned species is known for its determination and mental discipline, which enables individuals to tolerate great physical suffering.

Jedi tunic

Traditional leather utility belt

Long, loose robes

DURING the Clone Wars, Eeth Koth is taken hostage by General Grievous. Despite being captured, Koth is able to send a message to the Jedi Council revealing his location. Obi-Wan Kenobi and Adi Gallia stage a daring rescue and successfully retrieve the imprisoned Jedi Master.

Loose sleeves allow freedom of movement

Koth and his fellow Jedi must judge whether Anakin should start training.

Late Starter

Koth started his Jedi training at the unusually late age of four years, making him more receptive than his fellow council members to Qui-Gon Jinn's appeal to train Anakin Skywalker.

ELLO ASTY

RESISTANCE PILOT

DATA FILE

AFFILIATION: Resistance
HOMEWORLD: Unknown
SPECIES: Abednedo
HEIGHT: 1.88m (6ft 2in)
APPEARANCES: VII
SEE ALSO: Snap Wexley;
Poe Dameron; Jess Pava;
Nien Nunb

A SKILLED—if slightly impulsive—X-wing fighter pilot serving with the Resistance, Ello Asty flies with Blue Squadron during the battle to destroy the Starkiller.

"Pull to inflate"

Flight gauntlets

Life-support unit

Ejection harness

ASTY'S FLIGHT gear is the Resistance standard, though his helmet is specially fitted to his Abednedo head shape. He flew with Cobalt Squadron during the early days of the Resistance movement before eventually being reassigned to Poe Dameron's squadrons.

Top Gun

Ello is a masterful pilot behind the stick of a T-70 X-wing, a recent version of the famous rebel craft that flew at the Battle of Yavin. However, Ello struggles to be a team player in squadron maneuvers, as he is more inclined to fly alone.

EV-9D9

SADISTIC DROID SUPERVISOR

DATA FILE

AFFILIATION: Jabba's court
TYPE: Supervisor droid
MANUFACTURER: MerenData
HEIGHT: 1.9m (6ft 3in)
APPEARANCES: VI
SEE ALSO: C-3PO; R2-D2

EV-9D9 IS Jabba the Hutt's droid overseer in the murky depths of his palace on Tatooine. EV-9D9's programming is corrupted, and she works Jabba's droids until they fall apart, employing bizarre forms of droid torture to increase motivation.

EV-9D9 IS not the only EV unit with the programming defect that causes her cruel behavior. Many have the same flaw, but EV-9D9 was one of the few to escape the mass recall. EV-9D9 now relishes her role as taskmaster of all droids at the palace.

Degraded logic center

Manipulator arm

Supervisor

As Jabba's droid overseer, EV-9D9 assigns C-3PO as the Hutt's translator and R2-D2 as drinks waiter on Jabba's sail barge.

Custom-fitted third eye

EV-9D9 added a third eye to herself to "see" droid pain.

EVEN PIELL

LANNIK JEDI MASTER

DATA FILE

AFFILIATION: Jedi
HOMEWORLD: Lannik
SPECIES: Lannik
HEIGHT: 1.22m (4ft)
APPEARANCES: I, II, CW
SEE ALSO: Yoda; Anakin
Skywalker; Qui-Gon Jinn

Jedi topknot

THIS OUTSPOKEN JEDI MASTER is not to be underestimated. Even Piell bears a scar across his eye as a grisly trophy of a victory against terrorists who made the mistake of thinking too little of the undersized Jedi.

PIELL IS from Lannik, a planet with a long history of war. A gruff and battle-hardened warrior during the Clone Wars, Piell is taken prisoner and held captive at the infamous Citadel Station. Though mortally wounded during his escape, he is able to transfer vital information crucial to the war effort to Ahsoka Tano.

Large ears
sensitive in
thin atmosphere

Jedi robe

Seated next to Yaddle, Even Piell has one of the long-term seats on the Jedi High Council.

Momentous Events

Even Piell sits on the Jedi High Council during the galaxy's first steps toward war. He is present when Qui-Gon Jinn presents the young Anakin Skywalker to the esteemed Jedi leaders for the first time.

FIGRIN D'AN

BITH BAND LEADER

DATA FILE

AFFILIATION: Modal Nodes
HOMEWORLD: Bith
SPECIES: Bith
HEIGHT: 1.79m (5ft 10in)
APPEARANCES: IV
SEE ALSO: Jabba the Hutt

Enlarged cranium

Large eyes

Kloo horn

Tone mode selectors

A Wookiee named Chalmun owns the cantina in which the Modal Nodes often play.

DEMON KLOO HORN PLAYER Figrin D'an is the frontman for the Modal Nodes, a group of seven Bith musicians. They play in various venues on Tatooine, including Chalmun's Cantina in Mos Eisley and Jabba the Hutt's desert palace.

Band pants

FIGRIN IS a demanding band leader, who expects the best from his musicians. His overbearing nature has earned him the nickname "Fiery" Figrin D'an. As well as playing the kloo horn, Figrin is a compulsive card shark who frequently gambles the band's earnings.

Band Members

The Modal Nodes are Figrin D'an on kloo horn, Doikk Na'ts on Dorenian Beshniquel (or Fizzz), Ickabel G'ont on the Double Jocimer, Tedn Dahai on fanfar, Tech Mo'r on the Ommni Box, Nalan Cheel on the bandfill, and Sun'il Ei'de on the drums. Lirin Car'n often sits in to play second kloo horn.

Travel boots

FINN

STORMTROOPER DESERTER

DATA FILE

AFFILIATION: First Order/ Resistance

HOMEWORLD: Unknown

SPECIES: Human

HEIGHT: 1.78m (5ft 10in)

APPEARANCES: VII

SEE ALSO: Rey; Han Solo; Poe Dameron

Together Rey and Finn learn to trust each other as they flee their First Order pursuers, and embark into a wider galaxy of adventure.

Resistance fighter jacket, "borrowed" from Poe Dameron

A STORMTROOPER

who flees the First Order after a traumatizing first mission, FN-2187 finds a new home—and the name Finn—by joining the Resistance and helping in the mission to find Luke Skywalker.

Stormtrooper body glove

FN-2187 HAS

trained all his life to be an effective stormtrooper. He scored well in combat simulations, but during his first mission, he finds he does not have the brutal instinct to kill innocents in the name of the First Order.

Reckless Escape

Deserting from the First Order ranks, FN-2187 frees a Resistance prisoner, pilot Poe Dameron, who helps the fugitive stormtrooper escape from his Star Destroyer aboard a stolen TIE fighter. Poe gives FN-2187 the name "Finn." Crash-landing on the desert world Jakku, Finn's encounter with a scavenger named Rey will change the course of his life.

FIRST ORDER FLAMETROOPER

INCENDIARY WEAPONS STORMTROOPERS

DATA FILE

AFFILIATION: First Order
SPECIES: Human
STANDARD EQUIPMENT:
Flame projector
APPEARANCES: VII
SEE ALSO: First Order
snowtrooper; First Order
stormtrooper

FLAMETROOPERS are specialized stormtroopers of the First Order, who carry weapons that can transform any battlefield into an inferno. The First Order deploys flametroopers during the raid on Tuanul village on Jakku.

Conflagrine tank

D-93w flame projector gun

FLAMETROOPERS

carry D-93 Incinerators, a double-barreled flame projector that sprays an extremely flammable gel—conflagrine-14—from double storage tanks on the trooper's back. After being ignited electrically, the gel can be launched to a distance of 75 meters.

Flame-proof gaiters

Resistance soldier nicknames for flametroopers include "roasters," "hotheads," and "burnouts."

Flames of War

Flametrooper armor is reinforced cyramech that offers protection from heat, and the helmet's slit-visor reduces glare caused by intense flames. Flametroopers work alongside standard stormtroopers to methodically flush enemies from cover.

FIRST ORDER SNOWTROOPER

COLD WEATHER ASSAULT STORMTROOPERS

DATA FILE

AFFILIATION: First Order
SPECIES: Human
STANDARD EQUIPMENT:
Blaster rifle, blaster pistol
APPEARANCES: VII
SEE ALSO: First Order
flametrooper; First Order
stormtrooper

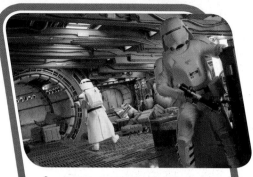

Snowtroopers examine the
Millennium Falcon after it
crash-lands on the Starkiller.

F-11D blaster rifle

Utility pouch

AS THE FIRST Order's
Starkiller operation is
based on an icy planet,
base security operations
are entrusted to the cold
weather divisions of the
stormtrooper ranks.

Insulating kama

SNOWTROOPER ARMOR offers more

mobility than the standard
trooper outfit, to make up for
the difficulties of snowbound
and icy terrain. Insulated fabric
covers most of the armor,
while a heating and personal
environment unit in the trooper's
backpack monitors and regulates
body temperature.

Ice Warriors

Aside from defending the Starkiller,
snowtroopers are tasked with the conquest
of icy worlds. The exposed sections of
betaplast armor are treated with a deicing
agent that prevents frost buildup. The helmet
visor is a minimal slit to reduce ice glare, and
heating filaments line essential equipment
to prevent freezing.

FIRST ORDER STORMTROOPER

LATEST GENERATION SOLDIERS

DATA FILE

AFFILIATION: First Order
SPECIES: Human
STANDARD EQUIPMENT:
Blaster rifle, blaster pistol
APPEARANCES: VII
SEE ALSO: Finn; Captain Phasma

Rank pauldron

Ammunition container

THE STANDARD INFANTRY of the First Order purposely resemble the feared soldiers of the Old Empire, which in turn were inspired by the clone troopers of the Republic.

FIRST ORDER

stormtroopers are trained from childhood to be soldiers. They undergo extensive combat drilling with detailed simulations to ensure a standard of excellence across their ranks, which far surpasses that of the Old Empire's stormtroopers.

The standard weaponry of the First Order stormtrooper is the versatile Sonn-Blas F-11D rifle, and the smaller Sonn-Blas SE-44C pistol.

Improved joint design

Into Battle

Ten standard infantry stormtroopers form the basic squad unit. One of those ten may also be a specialist trooper—a flametrooper, a stormtrooper equipped with an FWMB-10 megablaster, or a riot control stormtrooper.

FIRST ORDER TIE PILOT

DATA FILE

AFFILIATION: First Order
SPECIES: Human
STANDARD EQUIPMENT:
Blaster pistol
APPEARANCES: VII
SEE ALSO: Poe Dameron;
General Hux

Targeting sensors

Complete vac-seal helmet

Life-support gear

MODERN TIE PILOTS
benefit from the First
Order's increased focus
on the durability and
survivability of its
starfighter forces.
The new generation
of TIE fighter is much
better equipped
for combat.

The standard TIE fighter
craft of the First Order is
designated the TIE/fo.

WITH NO access to the
Empire's former academies, the
First Order instead trains its pilots
in secret aboard its growing
fleets of Star Destroyers. The new
generation of TIE pilots spend
most of their lives in space.

Positive
gravity
pressure
boots

Special Forces

A subset of the First Order TIE corps are the
Special Forces, identifiable by the red markings
on their helmets and ships. These are elite
pilots who fly a special two-crew version TIE
fighter with enhanced shields and hyperdrive.

FX-SERIES DROID

MEDICAL ASSISTANT DROIDS

Medical data banks

An FX-9 surgical assistant performs many blood transfusions during Vader's reconstruction.

High-speed data output transmitter

Equipment operator arm

MEDICAL DROIDS of all types are equipped with huge memory banks to allow them to choose the best course of treatment in any situation. FX-series droids act as medical assistants. They monitor patients and operate equipment.

Bioelectrical sensor arm

Pressure test arm

FX-SERIES droids have arms which can rapidly check the condition of a patient by performing various tests suited to different species. These droids work alongside surgeon droids, providing the surgeon with the information they need to perform appropriate treatments.

Life Saver

In the medical center within the rebel base on Hoth, an FX-7 med droid monitors Luke Skywalker's injuries while he is immersed in a bacta tank. The synthetic chemical bacta heals flesh wounds. FX-7 checks that the bacta mix is properly filtered and vitalized.

SENTRIES AT JABBA'S PALACE

DATA FILE

AFFILIATION: Jabba's court
HOMEWORLD: Gamorr
HEIGHT: 1.7m (5ft 7in)
APPEARANCES: CW, VI
SEE ALSO: Jabba the Hutt

Weak eyes

Fangs

TOUGH, BRUTISH Gamorrean guards stand throughout Jabba's Tatooine palace as sentries. These stocky, slow-witted, green-skinned creatures are stubborn and loyal, though prone to outbursts of barbaric violence.

Gamorreans are willing spectators to the casual violence at Jabba's palace.

Gauntlet

Heavy-duty ax

GAMORREANS

come from the warlike Outer Rim planet Gamorr. Male Gamorreans, called boars, either fight terrible wars or prepare for war, while the female sows farm and hunt.

Gamorreans are tasty treats for Jabba's rancor.

Leather sandals

Fit for Duty

The low intelligence of the Gamorreans makes them almost impossible to bribe, which is an asset to their masters. Their preferred weapons are axes and vibro-lances rather than blasters.

GARINDAN

MOS EISLEY SPY

DATA FILE

AFFILIATION: Various
HOMEWORLD: Kubindi
SPECIES: Kubaz
HEIGHT: 1.85m (6ft 1in)
APPEARANCES: IV
SEE ALSO: Sandtrooper; Luke Skywalker

GARINDAN IS A greedy and immoral Kubaz from the planet Kubindi. He is a paid informant who works for the highest bidder. In Mos Eisley, the Imperial authorities hire Garindan to locate two missing droids. The low-life spy quickly picks up the trail of Luke Skywalker, Obi-Wan Kenobi, R2-D2, and C-3PO.

On the Scent

Garindan discovers Luke Skywalker and his friends' plan to meet Han Solo at docking bay 94. Following the group, the sneaky spy then uses his Imperial comlink to call the authorities. When a squad of sandtroopers arrives, Garindan's job is done.

Garindan has a long trunk, which he uses to dine on his favorite delicacy: insects.

Dark goggles

Insect-eating trunk

THE MYSTERIOUS

Garindan keeps his face hidden behind a dark hood and goggles. Few individuals know anything much about his private life, which is also shrouded in secrecy.

Imperial comlink

GENERAL GRIEVOUS

COMMANDER OF THE DROID ARMY

DATA FILE

AFFILIATION: Separatists
HOMEWORLD: Kalee
SPECIES: Kaleesh (cyborg)
HEIGHT: 2.16m (7ft 1in)
APPEARANCES: CW, III
SEE ALSO: Count Dooku; Palpatine; Obi-Wan Kenobi

GENERAL GRIEVOUS is the Supreme Commander of the Droid Army during the Clone Wars. Grievous reacts furiously to any suggestion that he is a droid. In fact, he is a cyborg: a twisted mix of organic body parts and mechanical armor, with a hunched back and a bad cough.

Grievous's end comes when Obi-Wan Kenobi fires blaster bolts at his vulnerable gutsack.

GRIEVOUS IS a Kaleesh warlord who was rebuilt to increase his fighting prowess. The cyborg general is not Force-sensitive, but Darth Tyranus (Count Dooku) trained him in lightsaber combat.

Reptilian eyes

Cape contains pockets for lightsabers

Electro-driven arms can split in half

Grievous makes a daring assault on Coruscant in his flagship—the *Invisible Hand*.

Prepared for Battle

After their battle during the rescue of Palpatine, Obi-Wan Kenobi faces Grievous again in the Separatist base on Utapau. This time Grievous splits apart his arms in order to wield four lightsabers.

GENERAL HUX

FIRST ORDER OFFICER

DATA FILE

AFFILIATION: First Order
HOMEWORLD: Arkanis
SPECIES: Human
HEIGHT: 1.85m (6ft 1in)
APPEARANCES: VII
SEE ALSO: Supreme Leader
Snoke; Captain Phasma;
Kylo Ren; Finn

A YOUNG, ruthless officer in the First Order, General Hux has complete confidence in his troops, training methods, and technology. He relishes the opportunity to unleash the terrifying Starkiller weapon upon the galaxy.

Charcoal gray general's uniform

Polished officer's buckle

THE SON OF a prominent Imperial, Hux grew up celebrating the accomplishments of the Old Empire. He, like many in the First Order, believes that the New Republic are unworthy usurpers of power, and that the galaxy must be ruled with a strong hand.

Hux sees the Starkiller weapon as the ultimate expression of First Order doctrine—dominance through technological might.

Insulated boots

Hux and Kylo

Hux oversees the training of the First Order's stormtroopers, using a rigid program of simulations designed to hone military precision. A man who believes in results and data, Hux has little appreciation of the more mystical side of the First Order embodied by Kylo Ren.

GENERAL MADINE

DATA FILE

AFFILIATION: Rebel Alliance/
New Republic
HOMEWORLD: Corellia
SPECIES: Human
HEIGHT: 1.7m (5ft 7in)
APPEARANCES: VI
SEE ALSO: Mon Mothma;
Admiral Ackbar

AS COMMANDER of the Rebel Alliance Special Forces, General Madine devises the plan to destroy the Imperial shield generator on Endor's Moon. He also trains the strike force that infiltrates the Moon.

Command insignia

Rebel uniform jerkin

Briefing documents

Military gauntlets

General Madine helps Admiral Ackbar direct the Battle of Endor from the rebel flagship.

CRIX MADINE

led an Imperial commando unit until his defection to the Rebel Alliance. He is an expert in small ground strikes. Madine's unit of Alliance commandos was responsible for the capture of Imperial equipment and intelligence vital to crucial Alliance operations.

Rebel Advisor

Madine is a respected advisor to the rebel leader Mon Mothma. Before the Battle of Endor, Madine and Mothma brief their troops on board the Rebel Headquarters frigate, *Home One*. After the fall of the Empire, Madine commands the New Republic Special Forces.

GENERAL RIEEKAN

REBEL COMMANDER OF ECHO BASE

DATA FILE

AFFILIATION: Rebel Alliance
HOMEWORLD: Alderaan
SPECIES: Human
HEIGHT: 1.8m (5ft 11in)
APPEARANCES: V
SEE ALSO: Princess Leia

GENERAL CARLIST RIEEKAN is in charge of Echo Base on Hoth. He keeps the seven hidden levels of the base in a state of constant alert, ever wary of discovery by Imperial forces. Rieekan knows that any rebel activity could be easy to detect in the frozen Hoth system.

Rebel command insignia

RIEEKAN was born on Alderaan, Leia Organa's adopted planet. He fought for the Republic in the Clone Wars and became a founding member of the Rebel Alliance. Carlist is off-world when the Death Star superweapon destroys Alderaan, but this terrible event will haunt the rebel commander ever after.

Rieekan waits until all other rebel transports have left Hoth before escaping himself.

Utility belt

Insulated rebel uniform jacket

Command gauntlet

Stern Leader

Carlist Rieekan is a decisive commander. When the Imperial army discovers Echo Base, Rieekan plans to delay Vader's forces long enough to give the rebels time to evacuate the base.

GENERAL VEERS

DATA FILE

AFFILIATION: Empire
HOMEWORLD: Denon
SPECIES: Human
HEIGHT: 1.93m (6ft 4in)
APPEARANCES: V
SEE ALSO:
Admiral Piett;
Admiral Ozzel

GENERAL MAXIMILLIAN VEERS is cunning and capable. He has rapidly worked his way up the Imperial ranks. A family man, Veers is viewed as a model Imperial officer.

Blast helmet

GENERAL VEERS

is the mastermind behind the devastating Imperial assault on Echo Base—the Rebel Alliance base on Hoth. He commands the Empire's attack in person from within the cockpit of the lead AT-AT, codenamed *Blizzard One*.

Pilot armor

Utility belt contains
mission data

Imperial
officer's uniform

Cruel Ambition

Desperate to prove himself to Darth Vader, Veers heads the AT-AT regiment that successfully destroys the rebel shield power generator, allowing Vader to land on Hoth. Imperial snowtroopers, armed with heavy weapons, then infiltrate Echo Base with frightening speed.

General Veers takes aim at the rebels from inside the cockpit of his AT-AT.

GEONOSIAN SOLDIER

Prongs protect vulnerable blood vessels

DATA FILE

AFFILIATION: Separatists
HOMEWORLD: Geonosis
SPECIES: Geonosian
HEIGHT: 1.7m (5ft 7in)
APPEARANCES: II, CW
SEE ALSO: Poggle the Lesser; Count Dooku

Powerful sonic blaster

GEONOSIAN SOLDIER DRONES are tough and single-minded. They are trained to fight with a fearless attitude, and are highly effective against brute opponents. However, they are poor attackers when faced with intelligent enemies.

SOLDIER drones are grown to adulthood rapidly, and can be ready for combat at an age of only six years. They carry sonic blasters, which produce a devastating sonic ball.

Geonosians once numbered in the billions. They were practically wiped out after the completion of a secret Imperial construction project.

Soldier drones can fly or hover

Well-developed soldier's thigh

Red iketa stone traditionally associated with war

Like Geonosian blasters, the LR1K cannons rely upon sonic-based attacks.

Segregation

The caste-segregated planet Geonosis has become the chief supplier of battle droids to the Separatists, led by the aristocratic Count Dooku. Huge factories on Geonosis churn out countless droids.

ARCHITECT OF THE DEATH STAR

DATA FILE

AFFILIATION:
Republic/Empire
HOMEWORLD: Eriadu
SPECIES: Human
HEIGHT: 1.82m (5ft 11in)
APPEARANCES: CW, III, R, IV
SEE ALSO: Palpatine

Twisted, scheming gesture

AT THE END of the Clone Wars, Wilhuff Tarkin already has an exalted position as one of Palpatine's regional governors. As Grand Moff Tarkin, he plans the horrific Death Star as part of his doctrine of Rule by Fear.

Code cylinder

Tarkin dies on the Death Star when rebel X-wings cause it to self-destruct.

Imperial officer's disk

TARKIN has a history of quelling rebellion by the most cold-blooded means. He also created the role of Grand Moff—an official who has responsibility for stamping out trouble in "priority sectors" across the Empire.

Durasteel-toed boots

While there is friction between them, Vader always obeys Tarkin's commands.

Rule by Fear

In order to force Princess Leia to betray the Rebel Alliance, Tarkin orders the destruction of Alderaan by the Death Star. Rather than attempting to police all the scattered individual systems in the Imperial Outlands, Tarkin believes that fear of the Death Star will subjugate systems across the galaxy.

GREEATA

DATA FILE

AFFILIATION: Jabba's court
HOMEWORLD: Rodia
SPECIES: Rodian
HEIGHT: 1.7m (5ft 7in)
APPEARANCES: III, VI
SEE ALSO: Sy Snootles; Lyn Me; Rystáll; Max Rebo

Antennae detect vibrations

Flamboyant hairstyle decorated with feathers

Dancing costume

Suction-tipped fingers

Pheromone-suppressing bracelet

GREEATA JENDOWANIAN is a backing singer, dancer, and musician in the Max Rebo Band in Jabba's desert palace. Greeata forms a colorful alien trio with Rystáll Sant and Lyn Me.

GREEATA'S love of music and dance began as a youngster on her home planet of Rodia. She started out playing the kloo horn, and took a job on board a luxury liner, where she met fellow singer Sy Snootles. Together they formed a performing duo, which Max Rebo spotted playing in a cantina.

Singing for Hutts

Rystáll Sant, Greeata, and Lyn Me perform together at Jabba's palace. Graceful and rhythmic dancers make a powerful impression on the heavy, slow-moving Hutts. All the performers compete for Jabba's favor and indulgence.

Jabba's palace on Tatooine is hidden away in the Western Dune Sea.

GREEDO

RODIAN BOUNTY HUNTER

DATA FILE

AFFILIATION: Bounty hunter
HOMEWORLD: Rodia
SPECIES: Rodian
HEIGHT: 1.73m (5ft 8in)
APPEARANCES: CW, IV
SEE ALSO: Han Solo; Anakin Skywalker; Jabba the Hutt

Head spikes

Large eyes see in infrared spectrum

GREEDO IS A RODIAN bounty hunter who works for Jabba the Hutt. During the Clone Wars, he kidnaps Baron Papanoida's daughters, Che Amanwe and Chi Eekway. When Greedo demands debt payment from Han Solo in a Mos Eisley cantina, he finally meets his match.

GREEDO grew up on Tatooine and was known for his temper. He sometimes attempted to start fights with others, including Anakin Skywalker, who was then a slave in Mos Espa.

Blaster pistol

Well-worn flightsuit

Long, dexterous fingers

Greedo's End

The confrontation that takes place in the crowded cantina between Greedo and Han Solo begins with Greedo pulling a blaster on Solo. When Solo claims not to have the money on him, there is an exchange of blaster fire—and the Rodian falls dead on the table. Solo leaves, tossing a few coins at the bartender to hush up the incident.

GRUMMGAR

BIG GAME HUNTER

AFFILIATION: None
HOMEWORLD: Unknown
SPECIES: Dowutin
HEIGHT: 2.7m (8ft 10in)
APPEARANCES: VII
SEE ALSO: Bazine Netal;
Maz Kanata

A MERCENARY and big game hunter, the hulking brute Grummgar is obsessed with trophies. His bulky frame supports an enormous ego, and he doesn't realize that his partner, Bazine Netal, is a spy working him for information.

Hunting Grounds

Grummgar frequents Maz Kanata's castle, looking for hunting tips from the explorers who ply Wild Space and the Unknown Regions. Scouts' stories describing untamed worlds teeming with predators fill him with joy, and he returns from hunting expeditions with tales as tall as he is.

Plastoid armor plate

THOUGH unscrupulous, Grummgar avoids hunting intelligent prey—he prefers stalking wild animals to being a bounty hunter. That said, he will happily trample any rules that prevent poaching, and more than once he has pursued endangered animals on sacred grounds in pursuit of a rare trophy.

GUAVIAN SECURITY SOLDIER

ELITE CRIMINAL ENFORCERS

DATA FILE

AFFILIATION: Guavian Death Gang
SPECIES: Modified human
STANDARD EQUIPMENT: Percussive cannon
APPEARANCES: VII
SEE ALSO: Bala-Tik; Kanjiklub gang

Central sensor and broadcasting dish

Gorget armor

THE CYBERNETICALLY enhanced security soldiers of the Guavian Death Gang wear high-impact armor that makes them stand out among other deadly criminals. They are faceless, voiceless killers who show no mercy.

Percussive cannon

THESE MASKED soldiers communicate using high frequency signals that transmit from the disk in their faceplate. They are otherwise silent, giving them an even greater air of menace.

Ammunition pouch

Flexible armor shin guard

Illegal and Inhuman

A mechanical reservoir worn on the security soldier's leg acts as a second heart, injecting a secret mixture of chemicals that boost a Guavian's speed and aggressiveness. Coupled with the black market prototype weapons carried by the soldiers, everything about them is unnatural and dangerous.

HAILFIRE DROID

MOBILE MISSILE LAUNCHERS

HAILFIRE DROIDS roll rapidly into action, firing murderous explosive missiles from launcher pods. Their large hoop wheels move the droids at an intimidating speed. A red photoreceptor "eye" locks onto both land and air targets at impressive distances, giving the droids great reach.

Deadly Missiles

Hailfire droids have two racks of missile launchers on either side of their droid heads. Each rack carries 15 guided missile warheads. A single missile can destroy a gunship or AT-TE walker.

THE POWERFUL

InterGalactic Banking Clan uses hailfire droids to ensure its loans are paid back on time. During the Clone Wars, they donate these droids to the Separatists.

Hoop wheel

Missile rack

Photoreceptor

Hailfire droids, flanked by battle droids, roll toward the Republic Army on Geonosis.

AN SOLO

SMUGGLER AND WAR HERO

DATA FILE

AFFILIATION: Rebel Alliance/ Resistance
HOMEWORLD: Corellia
SPECIES: Human
HEIGHT: 1.8m (5ft 11in)
APPEARANCES: IV, V, VI, VII
SEE ALSO: Chewbacca; Princess Leia

Solo might be foolhardy, but he is courageous too—a match for any adventure!

Nerf leather jacket

HAN SOLO IS A pirate, smuggler, and mercenary. With his loyal first mate, Chewbacca, he flies one of the fastest ships in the galaxy—the *Millennium Falcon*. Han is reckless at times, but he proves himself a natural leader in the Rebel Alliance.

CHANGE is a constant in Solo's life. As a young man, he believed he made his own luck and was a man of few responsibilities. As he grows older and wiser, he has difficulty settling down to a life of peace. After suffering personal tragedy, Han once again returns to a reckless life in the criminal underworld.

Action boots

Strike Force

Han Solo leads a group of rebels, including Chewbacca and Leia, in a risky mission on Endor's Moon to destroy the second Death Star's shield generator. Solo shows Leia that there is more to being a scoundrel than having a checkered past!

HAPPABORE

BEAST OF BURDEN

DATA FILE

HOMEWORLD: Various, including Jakku
HEIGHT: 2.3m (7ft 6in)
DIET: Omnivorous
HABITAT: Deserts, savannahs
APPEARANCES: VII
SEE ALSO: Bantha; reek

THE HAPPABORE is a hardy, thick-skinned creature that can adapt to a wide variety of environments. They can be found either hauling scrap or carrying royalty, depending on the planet.

Desert Survivor

The massive snout of the happabore constantly sniffs out its surroundings, compensating for the creature's weak eyesight. The happabore also has stiff plating on its forehead, allowing it to burrow deep into the ground for roots and water.

HAPPABORES have thick skin that can shrug off heat, and they can go for days without water thanks to inner reservoirs that can hold liters at a time.

Tough skin

Massive tusks

HOMING SPIDER DROID

SEPARATIST SPIDER WALKERS

DATA FILE

AFFILIATION: Separatists
TYPE: OG-9 homing spider droid
MANUFACTURER: Baktoid Armor Workshop
HEIGHT: 7.32m (24ft)
APPEARANCES: II, III
SEE ALSO: Dwarf spider droid

THE COMMERCE GUILD'S contribution to the Separatist ground forces is the homing spider droid. It is an all-terrain weapon capable of precise targeting and sustained beam fire from its laser cannons. This metallic walking monster is a real danger to Republic walkers and gunships.

In Command

Homing spider droids move swiftly over battlefields on their long, powerful legs. The homing spider droid's main weapon is a top-mounted laser cannon, with a smaller, anti-personnel cannon positioned below it.

Extension hydraulics

Armored body core

Homing spider droids patrol the lush vegetation of the Separatist stronghold on the planet of Felucia.

Homing laser

Parallax signal tracing dish

Ambulation motors

BEFORE THE start of the Clone Wars, the Commerce Guild uses its homing spider droids to intimidate and control other large corporations, and to enforce tribute payments. At this time, armies are illegal, but many giant corporations flaunt huge security forces composed of droids.

REBEL FOOT SOLDIERS

DATA FILE

AFFILIATION: Rebel Alliance
SPECIES: Human
STANDARD EQUIPMENT:
Tripod-mounted blasters;
thermal flak jackets;
anti-glare goggles
APPEARANCES: V
SEE ALSO: Rebel trooper

Anti-glare goggles

Thermal flak jacket

Binoculars

Rebel troops use tripod-mounted blasters at the Battle of Hoth.

REBEL SOLDIERS ARE a rag-tag bunch. Some are deserters from the Imperial forces but many more are young volunteers with little or no experience in combat. New recruits receive basic training in handling weapons, communications, and emergency medical relief.

REBEL troopers on the ice planet Hoth must adapt quickly to freezing temperatures and the constant risk of sudden evacuation. They are equipped with specialist snow gear, including thermal flak jackets and polarized anti-glare goggles.

Relocation

After the Battle of Yavin, the Alliance relocates its secret headquarters to Hoth. Anticipating an Imperial invasion, the rebels modify their weapons to function in the icy temperatures.

IG-88

HIDEOUS ASSASSIN DROID

DATA FILE

AFFILIATION: Bounty hunter
TYPE: Assassin droid
MANUFACTURER: Holowan Laboratories
HEIGHT: 1.96m (6ft 5in)
APPEARANCES: V
SEE ALSO: Boba Fett; Darth Vader

Heat sensor

Vocoder

Ammunition bandolier

IG-88 IS A HEAVILY armed assassin droid that offers his services to Darth Vader to capture the *Millennium Falcon* after the Battle of Hoth. Also known as a Phlutdroid, IG-88 is a battered mechanical that has earned a reputation as a merciless hunter.

IG-88 is obsessed with hunting and destroying, as a result of his incompletely formed droid programming. The IG-series was designed to have blasters built into each arm, but they were never installed.

A wrecked IG-88 droid is left for scrap in Cloud City after Boba Fett caught it trailing him.

Outlaws

IG-88 joins the motley assortment of human, alien, and droid bounty hunters on the deck of Darth Vader's ship, the *Executor*. IG-88 and Boba Fett are longtime rivals. Assassin droids like IG-88 were outlawed after the Clone Wars, but they continue to stalk the galaxy.

Pulse cannon

Acid-proof servo wires

IMPERIAL DROIDS

THE EMPIRE'S UTILITY DROIDS

DATA FILE

AFFILIATION: Empire
TYPE: Droid
MANUFACTURER: Industrial Automaton (R2-Q5)
HEIGHT: 1.09m (3ft 7in)
APPEARANCES: R, IV, V, VI
SEE ALSO: Interrogator droid; Imperial probot

Magnetic fault sensor

THE GALACTIC EMPIRE uses a range of droids with limited independence. They are either existing droids adapted for Imperial purposes, or specialized new forms, including spy droids and illegal interrogator droids.

MSE (or "mouse") droids carry messages and guide troops to assigned posts.

R2-Q5 is one of the many Imperial astromechs that patrol the corridors of the Death Star, doing maintenance and repair tasks. Many such droids are fitted with secret spy devices that allow human overseers to monitor personnel.

Motorized leg

Heat exhaust

Powerbus cable for tread

Spy Droid

Arakyd Industries produce RA-7 protocol droids specially for the Empire. Unlike most protocol droids, these have unpleasant personalities and are almost always used as spies.

IMPERIAL PROBOT

REBEL-SEEKING PROBE DROID

DATA FILE

AFFILIATION: Empire
TYPE: Probe droid
MANUFACTURER: Arakyd Industries
HEIGHT: 1.6m (5ft 3in)
APPEARANCES: R, V, VI
SEE ALSO: Interrogator droid; Darth Vader

INTELLIGENT AND EERIE Imperial probots, also known as probe droids, relentlessly search the galaxy for any signs of the Rebel Alliance. They float above the ground on repulsorlifts and silenced thrusters. Probots are armed with blasters for self-defense and can self-destruct if captured.

Transmitter dome

Holocam

Defense blaster

Reinforced joint

Manipulator limb

Hyperdrive pods carry probots to their destination planets.

Invasion

A probot sent out from the Star Destroyer *Avenger* detects the rebel base on Hoth, and sends its images of the power generators back to Darth Vader. The Dark Lord immediately prepares his Death Squadron for a full-scale invasion of the frozen planet.

AFTER THE

Battle of Yavin, when the Alliance destroys the Death Star, the Empire sends out thousands of probots into every corner of the galaxy to find the hidden rebel bases. The probots use their sensors to discover a location's secrets and communicate their findings to distant Star Destroyers.

IMPERIAL RED GUARD

PALPATINE'S SECURITY FORCE

DATA FILE

AFFILIATION: Republic/Empire
HEIGHT: 1.83m (6ft)
APPEARANCES: II, CW, III, VI
SEE ALSO: Palpatine;
Darth Vader

Full-face helmet with
darkened visor

Red Guards eventually come
to replace the blue-robed
guards of the Galactic Senate.

Force pike

Synthetic leather
combat gloves

Long robe conceals
hidden weapons

ROYAL, OR RED, Guards
are Emperor Palpatine's
personal bodyguards.
From the time of his
appointment to Supreme
Chancellor, these Guards
have accompanied
Palpatine at all times.

Confrontation

When Moff Jerjerrod and two
Red Guards attempt to deny
Darth Vader entrance to the
Emperor's throne room on the
second Death Star, Vader
Force-chokes the officer,
though not fatally.

RED GUARDS

use vibro-active force pikes,
which inflict precise and lethal
wounds. Palpatine keeps the
details of the Guards' training
in deadly arts a secret,
citing "security concerns."

JABBA THE HUTT

NOTORIOUS CRIME LORD

DATA FILE

AFFILIATION: Grand Hutt Council, Crymorah Syndicate
HOMEWORLD: Tatooine
SPECIES: Hutt
LENGTH: 3.9m (12ft 10in)
APPEARANCES: I, CW, IV, VI
SEE ALSO: Bib Fortuna; Salacious Crumb

THE REPELLENT CRIME LORD Jabba the Hutt commands an extensive criminal empire. He built his operation through a long history of deals, threats, extortion, murders, and good business sense. Now, Jabba lives a life of wickedness in his palace located on the remote desert world of Tatooine.

Hutt skin secretes oil and mucus

Muscular body can move like a snail

Princess Leia exacts the revenge that all Jabba's slaves have dreamed about.

Body has no skeleton

...er

...his throne, with his slaves and ...ts all around, Jabba presides over ... murderous depravity. Many bounty ...d hired thugs seek work here.

JABBA REIGNS as head of the Hutt Grand Council, one of the largest criminal empires in the galaxy. Jabba prefers Tatooine to Nal Hutta, so Gardulla the Hutt often serves as his representative on the council. During the Clone Wars, Jabba allows the Republic to use private Hutt hyperspace lanes in exchange for rescuing his son, Rotta, from kidnappers.

JAN DODONNA

REBEL COMMANDER ON YAVIN 4

DATA FILE

AFFILIATION: Rebel Alliance
HOMEWORLD: Commenor
SPECIES: Human
HEIGHT: 1.83m (6ft)
APPEARANCES: IV
SEE ALSO: Luke Skywalker; Princess Leia

GENERAL JAN DODONNA is a master tactician for the Rebel Alliance. He commands the assault on the Death Star in the Battle of Yavin. Dodonna identifies the supposedly invulnerable station's single flaw: a small thermal exhaust port that leads straight to the explosive main reactor.

JAN DODONNA offers his skill and expertise to the Alliance once the Empire comes to power. After the Battle of Yavin, Dodonna is instrumental in locating a new base for the Rebellion.

Rebel command insignia

Rebel tactician's uniform

Commenor-style belt buckle

Ground Support
During the strike on the Death Star, Dodonna provides the rebel pilots with ground support from Yavin. His strategy enables a fleet of 30 fighters to destroy a battle station over 120 kilometers (75 miles) wide.

General Dodonna briefs the pilots in the command room the rebel base on Yavin 4

INTERROGATOR DROID

IMPERIAL TORTURE DEVICES

DATA FILE

AFFILIATION: Empire
TYPE: Interrogation droid
MANUFACTURER: Imperial Department of Military Research
WIDTH: 30cm (12in)
APPEARANCES: R, IV
SEE ALSO: Princess Leia; Darth Vader

WHEN PRINCESS LEIA refuses to discuss the location of the hidden rebel base, Darth Vader brings in an interrogator droid or, more accurately, a torture droid. Illegal by the laws of the Republic, torture droids are technological horrors invented behind the curtains of Imperial secrecy.

Torture droids hover and spin on repulsors, while flexing their terrible pincers and needles.

Chemical torture turret

INTERROGATOR DROIDS

are completely without pity. They exploit every physical and mental point of weakness with flesh peelers, joint cripplers, bone fragmenters, electroshock nerve probes, and other unspeakable devices.

Sonic torture device

Drug injector

Hypnotic power strip

Undefeated

Princess Leia had hoped the rumors of such atrocities as interrogator droids were not true. Leia somehow maintains her resistance to the machine's manipulations, even when she is near the point of death from the pain.

Victim analysis photoreceptor

J'QUILLE

WHIPHID HUNTER

DATA FILE

AFFILIATION: Jabba's court
HOMEWORLD: Toola
SPECIES: Whiphid
HEIGHT: 2m (6ft 7in)
APPEARANCES: VI
SEE ALSO:
Jabba
the Hutt;
Princess Leia

Retractable eyes

J'QUILLE IS A BRUTAL Whiphid from the frozen planet Toola. He works as a bounty hunter for Jabba the Hutt, though he is really a spy for a rival crime lord. He plans to destroy the Hutt by poisoning his food.

Coarse fur

Whiphids are huge, furred beings from the planet Toola. They have powerful tusks.

Survivor

J'Quille witnesses and survives the battle at the Great Pit of Carkoon. When Princess Leia strangles Jabba the Hutt, J'Quille's own murderous plans are foiled.

J'QUILLE works for Jabba's main rival on Tatooine, Lady Valarian, a female Whiphid with whom J'Quille also had an affair. After he fails to destroy Jabba, Lady Valarian places a large bounty on J'Quille's head. Unable to leave Tatooine, he joins the B'omarr monks.

JANGO FETT

DATA FILE

AFFILIATION: Bounty hunter, Separatists

HOMEWORLD: Unknown

SPECIES: Human

HEIGHT: 1.83m (6ft)

APPEARANCES: II

SEE ALSO: Boba Fett

Eye sensor allows Jango to see behind him

Fett is an expert pilot and teaches his son Boba from an early age.

Segmented armor plate allows flexibility

Gauntlet projectile dart shooter

DESPITE HAVING no affiliation with Mandalore, Jango Fett wears the armored uniform that helped make the Mandalorians a dreaded name. During the Republic's final years, he is regarded as the best bounty hunter in the galaxy.

Fett in his ship, *Slave I*, blasts Obi-Wan Kenobi's Jedi starfighter in the Geonosis asteroid field.

Segmented armor plate

Lethal Opponent

In battle with Obi-Wan Kenobi, Fett launches himself into the air using his jetpack. He carries many weapons, Including knee pad rocket launchers, and wrist gauntlets that fire darts, whipcords, and blades.

FETT'S REPUTATION as a supreme warrior led the Kaminoans to recruit him for their secret army project: every clone trooper is a clone of him. Fett receives a lucrative amount of credits, but also requests one unaltered clone to raise as his son.

JAR JAR BINKS

Haillu (earlobes) for display

DATA FILE

AFFILIATION: Gungan Grand Army, Republic
HOMEWORLD: Naboo
SPECIES: Gungan
HEIGHT: 1.96m (6ft 5in)
APPEARANCES: I, II, CW, III
SEE ALSO: Qui-Gon Jinn; Padmé Amidala

JAR JAR BINKS is an amphibious Gungan from Naboo. During the invasion of Naboo, Jedi Qui-Gon Jinn runs into and rescues Jar Jar. Jar Jar becomes a general in the Gungan Grand Army, and then a Junior Representative in the Galactic Senate.

At first, clumsy Jar Jar proves more of a hindrance than a help at the Battle of Naboo.

During the Clone Wars, Jar Jar goes on many diplomatic missions to aid the Republic.

Cast-off stretchy Gungan pants

Powerful calf muscles for swimming

JAR JAR is well-meaning but accident-prone. This simple soul is elevated to a position in the Senate that may be beyond his abilities. Luckily for him, the Naboo value purity of heart over other qualifications to govern.

Tight trouser ends keep out swamp crawlies

Good Intentions

In Padmé's absence, Jar Jar represents Naboo in the Senate. With the best of intentions, Jar Jar sets in motion a new galactic era as he proposes a motion for Supreme Chancellor Palpatine to accept emergency powers to deal with the Separatist threat.

JAWA

ROBED METAL MERCHANTS

DATA FILE

AFFILIATION: None
HOMEWORLD: Tatooine
HEIGHT: 1m (3ft 3in)
APPEARANCES: I, II, CW, IV, VI
SEE ALSO: Tusken Raider; R2-D2

Heavy hoods protect from sun glare

Glowing eyes

Bandolier

Ionization blaster

JAWAS SCAVENGE scrap metal, lost droids, and equipment on Tatooine. When Jawas arrive to sell and trade at the edge of town, droids stay away and individuals watch their landspeeders extra closely. Things tend to disappear when Jawas are around!

TIMID, GREEDY

Jawas wear dark robes to protect them from Tatooine's twin suns. Their glowing eyes help them see in the dark crevices where they hide, and their rodent-like faces are remarkably ugly to non-Jawas.

Desert Find

Unlucky droids that wander off or get thrown out as junk are favorite targets for the Jawas. They carry any finds to their sandcrawlers, where a magnetic suction tube draws the captured droid into the bowels of these ancient mining vehicles.

Most Jawas patrol the dunes and dusty rocks in gigantic sandcrawlers.

JESS PAVA

RESISTANCE STARFIGHTER PILOT

DATA FILE

AFFILIATION: Resistance
HOMEWORLD: Dandoran
SPECIES: Human
HEIGHT: 1.69m (5ft 6in)
APPEARANCES: VII
SEE ALSO: Ello Asty;
Nien Nunb; Snap Wexley;
Poe Dameron

A YOUNG, brave pilot, Jess serves as Blue Three within the Resistance. She flies alongside Snap Wexley and Poe Dameron in the crucial mission against the First Order Starkiller weapon.

Insulated helmet

Inflatable flight vest

Color known as "Interstellar orange"

THE MASSIVELY understaffed Resistance requires each member to fill multiple roles. In addition to serving as a pilot, Jess also helps catalog the astromech droids at the D'Qar base.

Ejection harness

Tales of Legends

Like many in the Resistance, Jess idolizes the legendary pilots of the previous generation. She bravely flies into battle above the Starkiller, and, following in the footsteps of the rebel pilots of old, volunteers to continue the mission even in the face of overwhelming First Order defenses.

KANJIKLUB GANG

FRONTIER BANDITS

DATA FILE

AFFILIATION: Kanjiklub
SPECIES: Human
STANDARD EQUIPMENT:
Cobbled together
blaster weaponry
APPEARANCES: VII
SEE ALSO: Tasu Leech;
Razoo Qin-Fee

THE KANJIKLUB are inhabitants of the planet Nar Kanji who were once enslaved by the Hutt crime lords, but then rebelled and killed their oppressors. They are notorious bandits and pirates.

Boiler rifle

Padded armor

VOLZANG LI-THRULL carries a
Tibanna-jacked boiler rifle
—an overpowered blaster
rifle that uses an explosive
mixture of Tibanna gas to
double its firepower. It is
a dangerous and illegal
modification.

Weapons
concealed in
leg pouches

Deadly Fighters
During their enslavement by the Hutts,
the people of Nar Kanji developed martial
arts that used improvised weaponry.
The modern Kanjiklubbers celebrate
this history by outfitting themselves with
modified armor and weapons. These
gangsters are not to be taken lightly,
as Han Solo discovers when he becomes
deeply indebted to them.

KI-ADI-MUNDI

CEREAN JEDI MASTER

DATA FILE

AFFILIATION: Jedi
HOMEWORLD: Cerea
SPECIES: Cerean
HEIGHT: 1.98m (6ft 6in)
APPEARANCES: I, II, CW, III
SEE ALSO: Commander
Bacara; Yoda

Large brain supported by second heart

Logical and methodical, Ki-Adi-Mundi cannot forsee the unthinkable betrayal in store for the Jedi.

Cerean cuffs

CEREAN JEDI MASTER

Ki-Adi-Mundi has a high-domed head, which holds a complex binary brain. He becomes a Jedi General during the Clone Wars and fights on Geonosis, among other worlds.

Travel pouch

Into Battle

Ki-Adi-Mundi fights alongside Clone Commander Bacara in many battles, including the attack on Mygeeto. But when Order 66 is activated, the clone troops turn on him. He defends himself bravely, but is destroyed.

Cerean fighting boots

KI-ADI-MUNDI is a thoughtful Jedi who shows great skill and courage in battle. He finds the adventurous nature of Anakin Skywalker and Ahsoka Tano unusual.

Ki-Adi-Mundi is a well-respected member of the Jedi High Council.

KIT FISTO

NAUTOLAN JEDI MASTER

DATA FILE

AFFILIATION: Jedi
HOMEWORLD: Glee Anselm
SPECIES: Nautolan
HEIGHT: 1.96m (6ft 5in)
APPEARANCES: II, CW, III
SEE ALSO:
Mace Windu

JEDI MASTER KIT FISTO is a fierce fighter who joins the 200 Jedi that travel to Geonosis to rescue the captives from the deadly execution arena. During the Clone Wars, Fisto accepts a seat on the Jedi High Council and is a veteran of many campaigns.

Low-light vision eyes

Tentacles detect chemical signatures

AS AN amphibious Nautolan from Glee Anselm, Kit Fisto can live in air or water. His head tentacles are highly sensitive and allow him to detect others' emotions. This ability allows Fisto to take instant advantage of an opponent's uncertainty in combat.

Jedi robe

Fallen Jedi

Most Jedi are deployed on distant worlds, but Mace Windu manages to assemble a trio of celebrated Jedi, including Kit Fisto, to assist him in arresting Palpatine. However, few Jedi of Mace's generation have fought a Sith Lord, and Fisto falls to Sidious's blade.

Kit Fisto leads a special unit of clone troopers at the Battle of Geonosis.

KORR SELLA

EMISSARY TO THE NEW REPUBLIC

DATA FILE

AFFILIATION: Resistance
HOMEWORLD: Unknown
SPECIES: Human
HEIGHT: 1.65m (5ft 5in)
APPEARANCES: VII
SEE ALSO: Princess Leia;
Major Brance; Admiral
Ackbar; Admiral Statura

LEIA ORGANA'S confrontational approach toward the First Order has left her politically isolated. She relies on emissaries like Korr Sella for continued contact with the New Republic government.

Rank of commander

Resistance officer uniform

DRESSED IN THE uniform of a Resistance officer, Korr Sella is an uncomfortable reminder to New Republic pacifists that war is sometimes inevitable. Leia Organa's words of warning regarding the First Order have caused the New Republic to brand her a warmonger.

Confident stance

Voice of the Resistance

Korr Sella is the daughter of New Republic politicians, but came to believe in Leia Organa's cause. A skilled diplomat, Korr maintains a fragile channel of communication between the Senate and the Resistance. When circumstances look most dire, Leia sends Sella to the Republic capital on Hosnian Prime to ask the New Republic for help.

KYLO REN

DARK SIDE ENFORCER

DATA FILE

AFFILIATION: Knights of Ren/
First Order
HOMEWORLD: Unknown
SPECIES: Human
HEIGHT: 1.89m (6ft 2in)
APPEARANCES: VII
SEE ALSO: Supreme
Leader Snoke; Rey;
Han Solo; Luke Skywalker

Combat helmet

Unstable
plasma blade
matrix

A DARK-ROBED warrior strong with the Force, Kylo Ren commands First Order missions with a temper as fiery and barely contained as the power within his lightsaber.

Kylo Ren greatly admires Darth Vader and owns the Dark Lord's charred and melted helmet.

THOUGH KYLO can use the Force, he is no Jedi or Sith. He follows his own path, encouraged by Supreme Leader Snoke to use the heritage of both the light and dark sides. These contradictory disciplines create a great conflict within Kylo.

Mysterious Warrior

Kylo's helmet is based on the battle gear of the Knights of Ren, and his peculiar lightsaber is a modern creation in an ancient style. Its cracked kyber crystal can barely contain the energy coursing through it, and a pair of crossblades vent out the excess power, balancing the weapon.

LAMA SU

KAMINO'S PRIME MINISTER

Elongated bones allow limited flexibility in neck

Kaminoans fly on creatures called aiwhas between their cities. Aiwhas can fly and swim with equal ease.

Cloak of office

LAMA SU is Prime Minister of Kamino, where the clone army is being created. He met with Sifo-Dyas, the mysterious Jedi who placed the order for a clone army. Lama is not concerned with the use of the army, only of the financial benefit for his people.

Dexterous fingers

KAMINO IS a remote, watery planet, cut off from the larger arena of galactic events. Lama Su is only marginally interested in off-world politics, and focuses on the technical challenges of cloning a mass army.

Small feet adapted to firm Kaminoan seabeds and now to hard flooring

Grand Tour

Lama Su personally takes Obi-Wan Kenobi on a tour of the cloning facility. The Prime Minister is one of the few Kaminoans to have any contact with off-worlders. But he is still not entirely comfortable in their presence. He makes no mention of Kenobi's unfamiliarity with the project.

LANDO CALRISSIAN

BARON ADMINISTRATOR OF CLOUD CITY

DATA FILE

AFFILIATION: Rebel Alliance
HOMEWORLD: Unknown
SPECIES: Human
HEIGHT: 1.78m (5ft 10in)
APPEARANCES: R, V, VI
SEE ALSO: Lobot; Han Solo; Ugnaught

Tarelle sel-weave shirt

Royal emblems

Borrowed rebel blaster

Lando disguises himself as a lowly skiff guard at Jabba's palace to aid in the rescue of Han Solo.

DASHING LANDO CALRISSIAN

is a rogue, con artist, smuggler, and gambler, who won control of Cloud City in a game of sabacc. He has come to enjoy his newfound sense of responsibility as Baron Administrator.

LANDO'S Cloud City is a fabulous mining colony on Bespin. After leaving the city, Lando falls in with the rebels. He is promoted to General and still finds adventure, but now contributes his abilities to a greater cause.

After Han's capture, Lando joins Chewbacca to search for his old friend.

Betrayed

Calrissian is forced to betray Han Solo and his friends to Darth Vader in order to preserve Cloud City's freedom. When he learns that the Sith Lord has no intention of keeping his side of the bargain, Lando plots a rescue mission and escapes from the city he once ruled.

LIEUTENANT MITAKA

FIRST ORDER OFFICER

DATA FILE

AFFILIATION: First Order
HOMEWORLD: Unknown
SPECIES: Human
HEIGHT: 1.8m (5ft 11in)
APPEARANCES: VII
SEE ALSO: First Order TIE pilot; Finn; General Hux; Kylo Ren

DOPHELD MITAKA is an attentive young officer serving aboard the First Order flagship *Finalizer*. A top graduate in his Academy class, Mitaka is not prepared for Kylo Ren's unforgiving command style.

Rank cylinders

Polished belt clasp

THE FIRST ORDER

naval uniform is descended from the sharp, authoritarian styles worn by officers of the Old Empire. The charcoal gray fabric signifies naval service, while the flared breeches and stiff boots help in maintaining a rigid posture. The command cap carries the starburst symbol of the First Order.

Mitaka issues orders on behalf of General Hux to stop the escaping TIE fighter carrying Poe Dameron and FN-2187.

Tough Job

After failing to recapture the escaped prisoner Poe Dameron and deserter FN-2187, Mitaka continues to oversee the progress of search teams scouring the desert wastes of Jakku. Mitaka has the unenviable task of updating Kylo Ren on the search after the fugitives flee Jakku aboard the *Millennium Falcon*.

LOBOT

DATA FILE

AFFILIATION: Rebel Alliance
HOMEWORLD: Bespin
SPECIES: Human cyborg
HEIGHT: 1.75m (5ft 9in)
APPEARANCES: V
SEE ALSO: Lando Calrissian

Efficient and near-silent, Lobot is the ideal assistant to flamboyant Lando Calrissian.

City central
computer link

Belt projects
clear-signal field

LOBOT IS CLOUD City's Chief Administrative Aide. He keeps in direct contact with the city's central computer via cybernetic implants that wrap round his head. Lobot can monitor a vast array of details at once.

Fineweave
sherculién-cloth shirt

THE IMPLANTS in Lobot's brain allow him to process information at incredible speeds, and let him retain much of his personality. Unfortunately, during a botched heist with Lando, Lobot had to let the implants take complete control of his mind, and he became, forever, a machine-like assistant.

To the Rescue

Lobot has no special love for Palpatine's Empire. When Lando Calrissian turns against Darth Vader and decides to rescue Han Solo's friends, Lobot's connection to the central computers proves useful. In response to Lando's "Code Force Seven," Lobot arrives with Cloud City guards to free Leia, Chewbacca, and C-3PO.

LOGRAY

EWOK HEAD SHAMAN

DATA FILE

AFFILIATION: Bright Tree Village
HOMEWORLD: Forest moon of Endor
SPECIES: Ewok
HEIGHT: 1.32m (4ft 4in)
APPEARANCES: VI
SEE ALSO: Chief Chirpa

LOGRAY is an Ewok tribal shaman and medicine man. He uses his knowledge of ritual and magic to help and awe his people. The shaman still favors the old Ewok traditions of initiation and live sacrifice.

Churi skull

Logray and Chief Chirpa eventually persuade their tribe to join the rebels in their fight.

Staff of power

Striped fur

Honor Feast

Logray first decides that Han Solo, Luke Skywalker, Chewbacca, and R2-D2 will be sacrificed. They will be the main course at a banquet to honor C-3PO, who the Ewoks believe is "a golden god."

IN HIS youth, Logray was a great warrior. His staff of power is adorned with trophies, including remnants of old enemies. Logray is suspicious of all outsiders, an attitude reinforced by the arrival of Imperial forces.

LOR SAN TEKKA

WISE SURVIVALIST

A KEEPER of obscure information, Lor San Tekka has traveled the wilds of the galaxy in pursuit of ancient relics. His secret knowledge proves vital to the survival of the Resistance.

Chain of Wisdom

Lor witnessed the early life of Kylo Ren. Enraged at Lor reminding him of simpler, more tranquil times, Kylo slays the old man.

Gundark-hide survival belt

Desperate Times

General Leia Organa is desperate to contact Lor San Tekka, believing he may have information revealing the location of her brother, the last Jedi in the galaxy. She dispatches her best pilot, Poe Dameron, to find the old traveler at Tuanul village on Jakku.

IN HIS TRAVELS,

Lor San Tekka uncovered many fragments of ancient Jedi traditions that the Old Empire had worked so hard to destroy. When Luke Skywalker began researching Jedi history in the hope of restoring the Jedi Order, he learned much from Lor San Tekka.

LUGGABEAST

CYBERNETIC PACK ANIMAL

Rey's Rescue

Teedos use the scanners built into their luggabeasts to detect droid power signatures or other salvage worthy of interest. A Teedo riding a luggabeast nearly succeeds in claiming BB-8 after trapping the little droid in a net. Luckily Rey intervenes and saves the plucky astromech before it can be disassembled and its parts sold.

BEASTS OF BURDEN

found on frontier worlds like Jakku, luggabeasts are semi-mechanical creatures whose faces are forever hidden behind heavy armor plating. The Teedos of Jakku use them as mounts and pack animals.

Armored slit conceals natural eyestalk

Salvaged speeder bike saddle

A LUGGABEAST'S

mechanical enhancements increase the creature's endurance to well beyond natural levels, a vital feature on some of the inhospitable worlds at the edges of Wild Space. The luggabeasts of Jakku have eye-like scanners suited for finding electronic salvage.

Armored leg

LUKE SKYWALKER

THE LAST JEDI

DATA FILE

AFFILIATION: Jedi
HOMEWORLD: Tatooine
SPECIES: Human
HEIGHT: 1.72m (5ft 8in)
APPEARANCES: III, IV, V, VI, VII
SEE ALSO: Princess Leia; Han Solo; Yoda; Darth Vader

In close combat with Darth Vader, Luke discovers the truth about his father.

Tatooine farm tunic

Anakin Skywalker's lightsaber

Droid caller

Tool pouch

TATOOINE FARMHAND Luke Skywalker is thrown into a world of adventure when he discovers a secret message inside one of his new droids. Luke becomes a space pilot for the Rebel Alliance and fulfills his true destiny as a legendary Jedi Knight.

AFTER THE Empire is defeated, Luke undertakes much study, travel, and spiritual contemplation, before committing to pass his knowledge on to a new generation of Jedi students. The reestablishment of the Jedi Order, however, suffers a terrible setback with the coming of Kylo Ren.

Jedi Path

Luke first climbs into the cockpit of an X-wing in the attack on the first Death Star. Fighting for the Rebel Alliance in the years afterward, Luke becomes a great leader. Yoda helps to awaken Luke's Force abilities, and, as a Jedi, Luke faces the challenges of the Emperor and Vader, holding the galaxy's hope for freedom.

LUMINARA UNDULI

MIRIALAN JEDI MASTER

DATA FILE

AFFILIATION: Jedi
HOMEWORLD: Mirial
SPECIES: Mirialan
HEIGHT: 1.7m (5ft 7in)
APPEARANCES: II, CW, III, R
SEE ALSO: Barriss Offee

Traditional Mirialan headdress

Luminara Unduli serves on Kashyyyk until she is captured by clone troopers during Order 66.

Mirialan facial tattoo

Form III lightsaber position

BORN ON THE COLD, dry world of Mirial, Luminara Unduli joined the Jedi Order at a young age. She fights against Count Dooku's droid soldiers at the Battle of Geonosis and is one of the few Jedi to survive the onslaught. Unduli serves as a Jedi General in the Clone Wars.

Battle on Geonosis

Luminara Unduli and more than 200 other Jedi fight Count Dooku's army in the Geonosis arena. When Jedi Master Yoda arrives with the newly created clone army, Unduli quickly takes command of a unit of soldiers to wage war in a great land battle against the Separatists.

LUMINARA UNDULI dies in an Imperial prison on Stygeon Prime. The Grand Inquisitor uses rumors of her survival and the lingering Force presence of her remains to draw out Jedi survivors.

LYN ME

PERFORMER IN THE MAX REBO BAND

DATA FILE

AFFILIATION: Jabba's court
HOMEWORLD: Ryloth
SPECIES: Twi'lek
HEIGHT: 1.6m (5ft 3in)
APPEARANCES: VI
SEE ALSO: Rystáll; Greeata

Lyn Me travels the galaxy
with the Max Rebo Band.

Lekku (head-tail)

Sensua bindings

Elegant hand
position

LYN ME IS A TWI'LEK dancer
and backup singer in the Max
Rebo Band at Jabba's palace.
She studied Twi'lek dance and
quickly gained the attention of
Max Rebo, who is constantly
on the lookout for new talent.

LYN ME grew up on
the barren northern continent
of Ryloth, the Twi'leks'
homeworld. Her species
has suffered generations of
hardships, with many Twi'leks
being sold into slavery by
the criminal underworld
that exists in their culture.

Dance shoes

Rescued

Boba Fett saved the young Lyn Me and many
others from slavery. Her village elders had
pooled their meager resources to pay the
famed bounty hunter to exterminate the
slavers. As a result, Lyn Me hero worships Fett.
While dancing at Jabba's palace, she spots
Boba Fett, and makes plans to talk to him.

MACE WINDU

LEGENDARY JEDI MASTER

DATA FILE

AFFILIATION: Jedi
HOMEWORLD: Haruun Kal
SPECIES: Human
HEIGHT: 1.88m (6ft 2in)
APPEARANCES: I, II, CW, III
SEE ALSO: Yoda; Anakin
Skywalker; Palpatine

A master of Form VII combat,
Mace Windu is one of the
best living lightsaber fighters.

MACE WINDU IS a senior
member of the Jedi High
Council. His wisdom and
combat prowess are
legendary. Windu is somber
and cool-minded, but
he is also capable of
dramatic actions in
the face of danger.

Jedi utility belt

Coarseweave tunic

Gut Instinct

Mace Windu's suspicions about Chancellor
Palpatine are proven right when Anakin
reveals that Palpatine is a Sith Lord. Windu
takes immediate action, promising to take
Palpatine into Jedi custody dead or alive.

MACE is decisive and
perceptive. He is one of the first
Jedi to sense danger in Anakin
Skywalker and is quick to lead
a Jedi taskforce to Geonosis
when war preparations
are discovered there.

Tunic allows ease
of movement
in combat

During Mace's duel with Darth Sidious,
Anakin has to choose whether to betray
his teachings or help capture the Sith Lord.

Boots offer
excellent traction

MAGNAGUARD

GENERAL GRIEVOUS'S DROID BODYGUARDS

DATA FILE

AFFILIATION: Separatists
TYPE: Bodyguard droid
MANUFACTURER: Holowan Mechanicals
HEIGHT: 1.95m (6ft 5in)
APPEARANCES: CW, III
SEE ALSO: General Grievous

Primary photoreceptors

Mumuu cloak markings match those on Grievous's mask

GENERAL GRIEVOUS'S BODYGUARDS are built to the alien cyborg's own specifications and trained by him. MagnaGuards often fight in pairs and can adjust their combat styles to match those of their opponents. They are equipped with deadly electrostaffs, or grenades and rocket launchers.

Electrostaffs are resistant to lightsaber strikes

Cloak is combat-tattered

MAGNAGUARDS

replicate the elite group of warriors and bodyguards that would always accompany Grievous when he was a Kaleesh warlord. Other Separatist leaders, including Count Dooku, come to use the MagnaGuards as bodyguards or soldiers.

Battle-scarred legs

MagnaGuards use their electrostaffs to stun or kill opponents.

Double Trouble

Anakin Skywalker and Obi-Wan Kenobi fight two MagnaGuards, IG-101 and IG-102, on Grievous's command ship *Invisible Hand*, when they attempt to rescue Palpatine. Even when Kenobi slices the head off one of the droids, it uses backup processors to continue fighting!

MAJOR BRANCE

COMMAND CENTER OFFICER

DATA FILE

AFFILIATION: Resistance
HOMEWORLD: Rinn
SPECIES: Human
HEIGHT: 1.75m (5ft 9in)
APPEARANCES: VII
SEE ALSO: Major Ematt;
C-3PO; Admiral Statura;
Princess Leia

A COMMUNICATIONS officer based in the Resistance command center on D'Qar, Major Taslin Brance keeps the upper ranks informed of the changing fortunes of the Resistance, and the growing threat of the First Order.

Major rank badge, army service

Resistance operations tunic

WITH FEW resources, the Resistance relies on up-to-the-minute intelligence in order to best prioritize missions against the First Order. Dispatchers and comm officers like Brance monitor transmissions from across the galaxy, seeking patterns, clues, and signs of danger.

Brance knows that poor intelligence can cost lives, and works hard to avoid mistakes.

Bad News

During the search for Luke Skywalker, Brance grows weary of always passing bad news to General Leia Organa. It is Brance who updates Organa with news that Lor San Tekka has been killed, and that Poe Dameron is missing and believed dead in the same First Order raid. He also reports on the first firing of the massive Starkiller weapon.

MAJOR EMATT

DATA FILE

AFFILIATION: Resistance
HOMEWORLD: Unknown
SPECIES: Human
HEIGHT: 1.8m (5ft 11in)
APPEARANCES: VII
SEE ALSO: Major Brance;
Han Solo; C-3PO; Admiral
Statura; Princess Leia

Major rank badge,
army service

Resistance shoulder
emblem

A VETERAN of the Rebel Alliance, Major Ematt was one of the first officers to join General Leia Organa's cause in the Resistance. He is an experienced soldier who is well traveled across the galaxy.

Resistance operations tunic

DURING THE Galactic Civil War, Ematt served as leader of the Shrikes, a special reconnaissance team responsible for identifying, securing, and preparing new locations to serve as safe zones for the Rebel Alliance.

Resistance Recruiter

In the early days of the Resistance, Ematt served as an agent for General Organa. He continued to serve in the New Republic military while seeking out potential converts for Resistance service. After the defection of too many New Republic pilots to go unnoticed, Ematt himself left his New Republic post to fully serve the Resistance.

MALAKILI

KEEPER OF JABBA'S RANCOR

JABBA'S CHIEF ANIMAL HANDLER, Malakili, looks after a murderous rancor that Jabba keeps beneath his throne room. Jabba loves throwing anyone who displeases him into the rancor's den, and Malakili tends any wounds that the monster receives from its unwilling snacks.

MALAKILI once worked as an animal handler in a traveling circus. When one of his dangerous beasts escaped during a show on Nar Shaddaa and killed audience members, Malakili was enslaved. After this incident, Malakili was sold to Jabba the Hutt.

Sweat-soaked rag belt

Wrist guard

Ancient circus pants

Jabba's rancor once saved Malakili's life when Sand People attacked him.

Beloved Pet

Both Malakili and his fellow animal handler, Giran, are very fond of the rancor that they care for. It is their favorite animal in Jabba's palace. Luke Skywalker slays the brutal beast after it attempts to devour him, and Malakili and Giran weep openly.

MAS AMEDDA

CHAGRIAN SENATE SPEAKER

DATA FILE

AFFILIATION: Republic/Empire
HOMEWORLD: Champala
SPECIES: Chagrian
HEIGHT: 1.96m (6ft 5in)
APPEARANCES: I, II, CW, III
SEE ALSO: Palpatine

Attack and display horns

Speaker's staff

MAS AMEDDA IS SPEAKER of the Galactic Senate on Coruscant where he keeps order in debates. Amedda is a stern and stoic Chagrian, and is one of a select few who understand that Palpatine is more than he appears to be.

Blue skin screens out harmful radiation

Robes of state

Amedda is the first to suggest that the Senate should give Palpatine emergency powers.

DURING Valorum's term as Supreme Chancellor, Mas Amedda is Vice Chair of the Galactic Senate. Secretly working for Palpatine, Amedda does everything in his power to tie up the Senate in endless debates so that Valorum loses the support of many Senators.

Standing Firm

Mas Amedda is by Palpatine's side after the fight with Yoda in the Senate, when Palpatine's personal shock troopers search for signs of the Jedi Master. After Palpatine transforms the Republic into the Galactic Empire, Amedda serves as his Grand Vizier.

MAX REBO

LEADER OF JABBA'S HOUSE BAND

DATA FILE

AFFILIATION: Jabba's court
HOMEWORLD: Orto
SPECIES: Ortolan
HEIGHT: 1.5m (4ft 11in)
APPEARANCES: VI
SEE ALSO: Sy Snootles; Droopy McCool

THE BLUE ORTOLAN, known in the entertainment business as Max Rebo, is a half-insane keyboard player who is completely obsessed with food. When the pleasure-loving crime boss Jabba the Hutt offers Max a contract that pays only in free meals, he immediately accepts—to the outrage of his bandmates!

Signed

Jabba is so enthusiastic about the wild music that the Max Rebo Band plays, he offers the band a lifetime gig at his palace. The band is playing when Luke Skywalker enters the palace to try to free Han Solo. After Jabba's death, the band breaks up.

Output speaker

Ears store fat

Air intake

Articulated toes can absorb food and drink

FOR AN

Ortolan, Max Rebo is quite skinny. His obsession with food may lead him to have poor judgment as the leader of his band, but he is devoted to music and quite good at his chosen instrument— the red ball jet organ.

Max Rebo's band accompanies Jabba's entourage on the Hutt's sail barge.

MAZ KANATA

DATA FILE

Affiliation: Pirate
Homeworld: Takodana
Species: Unknown
Height: 1.24m (4ft 1in)
Appearances: VII
See Also: Han Solo; Princess Leia; Rey; Finn

Variable lens corrective goggles

A MISCHIEVOUS PIRATE boss who has spent centuries surviving in the galaxy's fringe, Maz is regarded with respect by some of the toughest gangsters in space. Maz has a strong connection to the Force, but she is no Jedi.

Clothes knitted by Maz herself

Bracelet of the Sutro

MAZ'S HOSPITALITY

is legendary, and she invites independent starship crews to visit her castle keep on Takodana. As long as guests don't cause trouble, and grudges and politics are left at the door, Maz is happy to host all manner of low-bending wanderers in her home.

Scoundrel's Reunion

Han Solo has known Maz Kanata for decades, and describes her as an "acquired taste." Though she is small, Maz has a big and playful personality, passing on her wisdom with equal parts good humor and stinging criticism. Solo visits Maz after an absence of 25 years, to get help finding the Resistance. As Solo brings with him two fugitives from the First Order, evil forces close in and the Resistance soon comes to him.

ME-8D9

ANCIENT PROTOCOL DROID

DATA FILE

AFFILIATION: None
HOMEWORLD: Takodana
MANUFACTURER: Unknown
HEIGHT: 1.72m (5ft 8in)
APPEARANCES: VII
SEE ALSO: Maz Kanata;
Bazine Netal

KNOWN AS "Emmie" to the scoundrels within Maz's castle on Takodana, ME-8D9 is a protocol droid who is often called on to translate the less-than-legal deals made within the castle's dining and gaming halls.

Shielded data
storage center

Bronzium-enriched finish

EMMIE IS an ancient droid of an unknown model, and rumor has it that she is as old as the castle itself. Emmie has little memory of her original functions, and she has been reprogrammed countless times.

Knee assembly

Reinforced ankle joint

Mysterious Past

Fragments of Emmie's past surface occasionally—a side-effect of her outdated design. Though mainly built for protocol duty, she has also served as an assassin for shady criminals, including the notorious Crymorah. There are some who believe she was originally in the service of the ancient Jedi Order.

MOFF JERJERROD

SUPERVISOR OF THE SECOND DEATH STAR

DATA FILE

AFFILIATION: Empire
HOMEWORLD: Tinnel IV
SPECIES: Human
HEIGHT: 1.73m (6ft)
APPEARANCES: VI
SEE ALSO: Darth Vader;
Captain Needa

MOFF JERJERROD SUPERVISES the construction of the second Death Star. During the Battle of Endor, Jerjerrod commands the station's superlaser against the rebel forces. He is killed when the rebels finally detonate the Death Star's reactor.

Imperial code cylinder

Rank insignia plaque

Imperial officer's tunic

Jerjerrod blames slow progress of the Death Star's construction on a shortfall of workers.

JERJERROD was born to a wealthy family on the Core World of Tinnel IV. He shows petty spitefulness and a lack of ambition as he rises through the Imperial ranks—both admirable qualities in a Moff. When he is assigned to the top secret second Death Star project, his cover title is Director of Imperial Energy Systems.

Naval boots

Called to Account

When the construction of the Death Star falls behind schedule, the Emperor sends Vader to put additional pressure on Moff Jerjerrod and his construction crews. Informed that the Emperor himself will soon be arriving, Jerjerrod assures Vader his men will double their efforts.

MON MOTHMA

REBEL ALLIANCE LEADER

DATA FILE

AFFILIATION: Republic/Rebel Alliance/New Republic
HOMEWORLD: Chandrila
SPECIES: Human
HEIGHT: 1.73m (5ft 8in)
APPEARANCES: CW, III, VI
SEE ALSO: Bail Organa

Simple Chandrilan hairstyle

MON MOTHMA IS THE highest leader of the Rebellion. As a member of the Galactic Senate, she champions the cause of freedom until the Emperor's evil closes in around her. Abandoning the Senate, Mothma works with Bail Organa to form the Rebel Alliance that aims to unseat the Galactic Empire.

Hanna pendant

Elegant robe of Fleuréline weave

Gesture of reconciliation

After the fall of the Empire, Mothma will become the New Republic's first Chancellor.

Shraa silk mantle

MON MOTHMA was born into a political family and became the youngest Senator to enter the Senate. When the Republic collapses, she goes underground and begins to organize the various cells of resistance into a single entity: The Alliance to Restore the Republic (or Rebel Alliance).

Rebel Founders

Mon Mothma and Bail Organa become convinced that Palpatine needs to be opposed. With the the Senate under Palpatine's control, and his newly appointed governors overseeing all star systems, the two loyalists make a pact with a few dependable Senators to form a highly secret Rebellion movement.

MUFTAK

MOS EISLEY CANTINA PATRON

DATA FILE

AFFILIATION: None
HOMEWORLD: Orto Plutonia
SPECIES: Talz
HEIGHT: 2.1m (6ft 11in)
APPEARANCES: IV
SEE ALSO: Figrin D'an

MUFTAK IS A TALZ pickpocket who lives in abandoned tunnels beneath Mos Eisley. He is a regular in the booths of Chalmun's Cantina. He is drinking there on the day that Obi-Wan Kenobi and Luke Skywalker arrive in search of a spacer who will agree to take them off-world.

Criminal Activities

Muftak is friends with various regulars at Chalmun's Cantina. When not drinking, he plans robberies with a Chadra-Fan named Kabe. Though Kabe is street-smart, she is also a young and impetuous. Muftak takes it upon himself to use his great strength to keep her out of too much trouble.

Day vision eyes
(night vision
eyes beneath)

TALZ ARE a primitive species from Orto Plutonia who use few tools. Muftak was abandoned in Mos Eisley as a newborn. He grew up knowing he was different from other species, but had no knowledge of the Talz or his homeworld.

Sharp talons

Muftak's thick fur protects his species from the frozen climate of its homeworld.

Proboscis for
feeding and
communicating

MUSTAFARIANS

MUSTAFAR'S MINERS

THE TWO DISTINCT species of Mustafarians (Northern and Southern) evolved separately in underground caves. They work together to collect valuable minerals from the lava flow, and have a trade agreement with the Techno Union.

SOUTHERN MUSTAFARIANS are
stockier and stronger than their Northern counterparts. While their tough skin can resist higher temperatures, even they have to wear insulated armor when working close to the lava flows.

Shock-resistant exoskeleton

Eyes distinguish between light and darkness

Breath mask

Powerful legs for jumping

NORTHERN MUSTAFARIANS
have less resistance than the Southern species to the lava streams' high temperatures, so they generally wear insulated armor and ride lava fleas.

Lava-resistant cauldron

NABOO GUARD

DATA FILE

AFFILIATION: Royal Naboo Security Forces
HOMEWORLD: Naboo
SPECIES: Human
APPEARANCES: I, II, CW
SEE ALSO: Captain Panaka

THE NABOO ROYAL GUARD is the highly trained bodyguard of the Naboo monarch and court. Its loyal, dedicated soldiers typically experience battle off-planet and return to Naboo to protect the royal house out of loyalty.

Naboo forces use small Gian landspeeders in their attempt to repel the invading droid army.

Blast-damping armor

Unarmored joints for agility

Utility belt

No leg armor for mobility

THE ROYAL GUARD

forms one component of the Naboo Royal Security Forces. Its members work alongside the Security Guard, which comprises mainly sentries and patrolmen, and the Space Fighter Corps, which flies N-1 starfighters.

Shin protectors

Returning Forces

When the Trade Federation droid army invades Naboo, the Royal Guard gets its first taste of true battle. But the sheer number of battle droids means a defeat for Naboo. Fortunately, Queen Amidala and Head of Security, Captain Panaka, escape and are able to return, with the Gungans, to put an end to the droid occupation.

NABOO SEA MONSTERS

CREATURES OF THE DEEP

NABOO SEA MONSTERS

DATA FILE

HOMEWORLD: Naboo
AVERAGE SIZE: Various
DIET: Carnivorous
HABITAT: Lakes, seas, oceans
APPEARANCES: 1
SEE ALSO: Jar Jar Binks

THE FABLED sando aqua monster is rarely seen in Naboo's oceans and lakes, despite its monstrous size. This creature swims using its long powerful tail and massive flippers. It has clawed hands, which it uses to grasp prey. Male sando aqua monsters can grow up to 200 meters (656 feet) in length.

Sharp teeth

Lure

Webbed claws allow creature to grab its prey

IN THE MURKY

waters of Naboo's underground lakes, the opee sea killer lurks within dark caverns. This monster waits motionless, using a long antenna-like lure on its head to attract the attention of its prey. It gives pursuit using its tail legs and jet propulsion vents to swim at great speed towards it prey.

THE COLO

claw fish, found in lakes on Naboo, is adapted to swallow prey larger than its own head. Its jaws can distend and its skin can stretch to engulf astonishingly large creatures. This serpentine predator digests its food slowly, using weak stomach acids.

Venomous fangs

Nodules attract prey

NEXU

FANGED ARENA BEASTS

DATA FILE

HOMEWORLD: Cholganna
AVERAGE SIZE: 1m (3ft) high, 2m (6ft 7in) long
DIET: Carnivorous
HABITAT: Forests
APPEARANCES: II
SEE ALSO: Padmé Amidala; acklay; reek

A NEXU IS ONE OF THE savage beasts let loose on condemned prisoners in the Geonosian arenas, for the amusement of an enthusiastic crowd. The nexu is native to Cholganna, where it lives and hunts in cool forests. Its secondary eyes see in infrared wavelengths, allowing it to spy the heat signatures of warm-blooded prey.

Goaded into Action

A Geonosian picador on a tame orray mount prods the nexu with his static pike to goad the beast into the arena. The picador must be careful to avoid the nexu turning round suddenly, because the sharp spines on its back can inflict deadly wounds.

The nexu seizes prey in its fanged mouth, then shakes or bites the creature to death.

Quills erect in combat

Secondary eyes for heat vision

THE NEXU is set on condemned prisoners Anakin Skywalker, Obi-Wan Kenobi, and Padmé Amidala. Padmé climbs an execution pillar to escape its savage jaws, and uses her own chains to keep it at bay. But it takes a charging reek, ridden by Anakin, to finally flatten the beast.

Fangs in wide mouth

Hind-leg claws

NIEN NUNB

HEROIC SULLUSTAN PILOT

DATA FILE

AFFILIATION: Rebel Alliance/Resistance
HOMEWORLD: Sullust
SPECIES: Sullustan
HEIGHT: 1.79m (5ft 10in)
APPEARANCES: VI, VII
SEE ALSO: Lando Calrissian

NIEN NUNB is Lando Calrissian's Sullustan copilot on board the *Millennium Falcon* at the Battle of Endor. Lando understands the Sullustan language that Nien speaks, and personally picks him for the mission, impressed by Nien's exploits aboard his own renowned vessel, the *Mellcrawler*.

Tool pouch

Pressurized g-suit

Gear harness

Flight gauntlets

NIEN NUNB is one of many Sullustans who serve as fighter pilots in the Rebel Alliance. His homeworld, Sullust, is the staging area for the rebel fleet before the Battle of Endor. The Alliance award Nunb a medal named the Kalidor Crescent for his bravery in the battle.

Nunb and Calrissian pilot the *Falcon* through the Death Star's unfinished superstructure.

Positive-grip boots

Trusted Pilot

Nunb learned his piloting skills flying a freighter for the Sullustan SoroSuub Corporation. When SoroSuub begins to support the Empire, Nunb shows his opposition by stealing from the company on behalf of the Rebel Alliance. At first, Nunb works as an independent smuggler, but he eventually becomes a full-time member of the Alliance.

NUTE GUNRAY

NEIMOIDIAN VICEROY

DATA FILE

AFFILIATION: Trade Federation, Separatists
HOMEWORLD: Neimoidia
SPECIES: Neimoidian
HEIGHT: 1.91m (6ft 3in)
APPEARANCES: I, II, CW, III
SEE ALSO: Palpatine; Padmé Amidala

Viceroy's crested tiara

THE VICEROY OF THE Trade Federation, Nute Gunray is powerful, deceitful, and willing to kill for his far-reaching commercial aims. Gunray becomes an unwitting pawn of Darth Sidious when he agrees to invade the peaceful planet of Naboo.

Wheedling expression

Viceroy's collar

The Trade Federation secretly aids the Separatists during the Clone Wars.

Sidious will need the Trade Federation's help only until his control of the galaxy is assured.

NUTE GUNRAY

is a Neimoidian, a species known for its exceptional greed. Gunray makes an alliance with Darth Sidious to blockade Naboo in opposition to increased taxation. However, Gunray feels increasingly uneasy when his alliance with Sidious leads to open warfare.

True Face

Gunray's true cowardice shows itself when Padmé Amidala's freedom fighters storm the Royal Palace. Unable to hide behind battle droids any longer, Gunray is arrested. It is a sign of the Republic's decay that he is later able to buy his release and continue as Viceroy of the Trade Federation.

OBI-WAN KENOBI

LEGENDARY JEDI MASTER

DATA FILE

AFFILIATION: Jedi
HOMEWORLD: Stewjon
SPECIES: Human
HEIGHT: 1.79m (5ft 10in)
APPEARANCES: I, II, CW, III, R, IV, V, VI
SEE ALSO: Anakin Skywalker; Luke Skywalker

Under-tunic

Jedi robe

Kenobi faces Darth Vader—once Kenobi's Padawan, Anakin Skywalker—in battle.

Kenobi's lightsaber skills are legendary

OBI-WAN KENOBI is a truly great Jedi who finds himself at the heart of galactic turmoil as the Republic unravels and finally collapses. Although cautious by nature, Kenobi has a healthy independent streak and truly formidable lightsaber skills.

KENOBI'S path is destined to lead in a very different direction to that of his Jedi partner, Anakin Skywalker. After Order 66, Kenobi helps protect Luke and Leia Skywalker. For many years, he remains in hiding on Tatooine, watching over Luke Skywalker, the last hope for the ancient Jedi Order.

Obi-Wan's considered approach to situations often conflicts with Anakin's brash nature.

General Kenobi

Kenobi becomes a great Jedi General and pilot in the Clone Wars (despite being a reluctant flier!). Trained by the headstrong Qui-Gon Jinn, Kenobi trains his own master's protégé, Anakin Skywalker, after Jinn's death. The bond between Obi-Wan and Anakin is strong as they fight through the Clone Wars.

OCTUPTARRA DROID

TECHNO UNION BATTLE DROIDS

DATA FILE

AFFILIATION: Separatists
TYPE: Octuptarra combat tri-droid
MANUFACTURER: Techno Union
HEIGHT: 3.6m (11ft 10in)
APPEARANCES: CW, III
SEE ALSO: Crab droid

OCTUPTARRA DROIDS are terrifying three-legged battle droids manufactured by the Techno Union. The droids have rotating laser turrets which can spin round to lock onto targets from any side in an instant. This makes them almost impossible for enemy troops to attack by surprise from behind.

Battle on Utapau

On Utapau, octuptarra droids protect General Grievous's headquarters from oncoming clone troopers. However, Clone Commander Cody's 212th Attack Batallion continues to push forward, at least until the initiation of Order 66 refocuses their priorities and they turn on the Jedi.

After the establishment of the Empire, most octuptarra droids are deactivated.

Cognitive module and sensor suite

Rotating laser turret

Triple-jointed hydraulic limbs

OCTUPTARRA

droids are named for the eight-eyed, gasbag-headed vine walkers found on Skako. The largest models are used as combat artillery, while agile battle droid-sized versions are used as antipersonnel weapons.

OOLA

TWI'LEK DANCER

DATA FILE

AFFILIATION: Jabba's court
HOMEWORLD: Ryloth
SPECIES: Twi'lek
HEIGHT: 1.6m (5ft 3in)
APPEARANCES: VI
SEE ALSO: Jabba the Hutt

OOLA IS A green-skinned Twi'lek dancer enslaved to the cruel crime lord Jabba the Hutt. Jabba's major-domo, Bib Fortuna, kidnapped Oola from a primitive clan. He had other Twi'lek girls train Oola in the art of exotic dancing, so he could present her to his boss.

Lekku (head-tail)

Leather straps

Oola dances for her life in Jabba's palace, but ends up in the dreadful rancor pit.

Flimsy net costume

OOLA'S life is tragic and short. Enslaved by Bib Fortuna, a stranger offers her the chance to escape in Mos Eisley. However, Fortuna has fed her so many lies about the glory of Jabba's palace that she wants to see it for herself, so she refuses this opportunity to be free.

Gruesome End

Jabba lavishes particular attention on Oola, keeping her chained to his throne. However, when Oola once more refuses Jabba's advances, the revolting Hutt is infuriated. He opens the trap door beneath the dance floor and watches as Oola is fed to his deadly rancor monster.

OPPO RANCISIS

OPPO RANCISIS

JEDI HIGH COUNCIL MEMBER

DATA FILE

AFFILIATION: Jedi
HOMEWORLD: Thisspias
SPECIES: Thisspiasian
HEIGHT: 1.38m (4ft 6in)
APPEARANCES: I, II, CW
SEE ALSO: Yaddle

OPPO RANCISIS IS a Thisspiasian Jedi Master who sits on the Jedi High Council. He joined the Jedi Order as an infant, and trained under Master Yaddle. When offered the throne of Thisspias, he declined it to continue to serve the galaxy as a Jedi. He is now a top Jedi military advisor.

Dense hair deters biting cygnats of Thisspias

RANCISIS is an excellent strategist, who ensures that, if negotiation fails, Jedi-counseled military tactics are cunning and effective. During the Clone Wars, Rancisis fights in the Siege of Saleucami, but also spends much time on Coruscant, coordinating Republic forces throughout the galaxy.

Master Jedi

Rancisis is adept with his green-bladed lightsaber, but prefers to use his highly developed Force powers for combat. He is a formidable foe in unarmed combat, using his four arms and long tail to make surprising strikes at his opponent.

Second pair of hands hidden underneath cloak

Fingers tipped with claws

OWEN LARS

LUKE SKYWALKER'S GUARDIAN

DATA FILE

AFFILIATION: None
HOMEWORLD: Tatooine
SPECIES: Human
HEIGHT: 1.7m (5ft 7in)
APPEARANCES: II, III, IV
SEE ALSO: Beru Lars; Cliegg
Lars; Luke Skywalker

AS A YOUNG NEWLYWED,
Owen Lars made a huge decision.
He agreed to hide and protect a
baby from the wrath of his own
father: Darth Vader. The baby was
named Luke by his mother,
Padmé, moments before she
died in childbirth. Owen
gained a nephew, but
also added to his worries.

Rough clothing
made in Anchorhead

Simple overcoat
provides warmth in the
cold desert evenings

Tool pouch

YOUNG OWEN was
born to Cliegg Lars and his
first wife Aika. He has spent
most of his life on his
father's homestead on
Tatooine, which he inherited
after Cliegg passed away.
Owen falls in love with Beru
after meeting her in nearby
Anchorhead. It is Beru who
convinces the reluctant Owen
to adopt Anakin's son.

A Farmer's Life

When Luke has grown, he works
closely with Owen on the family
homestead. They maintain the
vaporators that collect precious
moisture from the desert air, and
buy "used" droids from passing
Jawas. Although the teenage
Luke is ready to fly the nest,
Owen finds it hard to shrug off the
gruff, protective attitude that has
become a habit over the years.

Owen, his wife Beru, and father
Cliegg met Luke's parents,
Anakin and Padmé, only once.

PADMÉ AMIDALA

NABOO QUEEN AND SENATOR

DATA FILE

AFFILIATION: Royal House of Naboo, Galactic Senate
HOMEWORLD: Naboo
SPECIES: Human
HEIGHT: 1.65m (5ft 5in)
APPEARANCES: I, II, CW, III
SEE ALSO: Anakin Skywalker; Captain Panaka

Hair pulled tightly back for clear view of enemy

Slashes in clothing sustained in Geonosian arena battle

PADMÉ AMIDALA HAS TIME and again found herself at the center of galactic events. From the invasion of her home planet, Naboo, to a death sentence in a Geonosian arena, by way of multiple attempts on her life as a Senator, Padmé faces extraordinary danger with determination and great bravery.

PADMÉ GREW

up in a small Naboo village. Exceptionally talented, she was elected queen at the age of only 14. At the end of her term of office, Padmé is made Senator of Naboo. It is on the Galactic capital, Coruscant, that she becomes closer to Anakin Skywalker.

Light shin armor

Action boots with firm grip

Padmé and Anakin surrender to the love they share, though they know it breaks Jedi rules.

Queen Turned Fighter

As the young Queen of Naboo, Padmé Amidala has to learn that her cherished values of non-violence will not save her people from a brutal droid invasion. Discarding her formal robes of state, Padmé determines to inspire her own troops to end the invasion by capturing the Neimoidian leaders.

PALPATINE

SITH LORD AND GALACTIC EMPEROR

DATA FILE

AFFILIATION: Sith, Republic/Empire
HOMEWORLD: Naboo
SPECIES: Human
HEIGHT: 1.78m (5ft 10in)
APPEARANCES: I, II, CW, III, R, V, VI
SEE ALSO: Darth Vader

Hood to hide face

PALPATINE is known by many names. Born on Naboo, Sheev Palpatine becomes his homeworld's Senator. Then, he is Supreme Chancellor Palpatine. Finally, he declares himself Emperor and rules the galaxy. Ultimate power has been his plan all along. Palpatine is secretly Darth Sidious, the most evil of Sith Lords.

Palpatine secretly plans the Clone Wars to destroy the Galactic Republic and the Jedi Order.

PALPATINE manages to keep all those around him from suspecting his true identity. For years, he has appeared patient and unassuming, so few have recognized his political ambitions. His dark side powers even blinded the Jedi from seeing behind his mask of affability.

Sensing Vader's defeat on Mustafar, Palpatine travels to his apprentice's side.

Sith Powers

His face twisted and scarred by the dark energies of the Force, Emperor Palpatine is a figure of terrible power. One of his most deadly weapons is Sith lightning, which is projected from his fingertips. A Force user can block the lethal energy for a while if they are strong, but it takes immense effort.

PIT DROID

DROID PODRACER MECHANICS

DATA FILE

AFFILIATION: None
TYPE: Repair droid
MANUFACTURER:
Serv-O-Droid
HEIGHT: 1.19m (3ft 11in)
APPEARANCES: I, II, CW
SEE ALSO: Podracers

Head plate protects against falling tools

BUSY, SLIGHTLY CLUMSY

pit droids work in pit hangars and race arenas on planets where the high-speed sport of podracing takes place. Pit droids assist with all podrace maintenance tasks and report to human podracer mechanics, who oversee complex decisions and custom engine modifications.

Monocular photoreceptor

Illegal frequency jammer

Hardened alloy casing

PIT DROIDS are programmed to take orders and carry them out as quickly as possible, without asking questions. Accordingly, their logic processors are quite basic. However, this can leave the droids confused about how to get a job done, causing mayhem in the process.

Power wrench

Jar Jar Binks finds out that pit droids pop open when tapped on the head.

Pit Droid Mishap

In the Boonta Eve Classic podrace on Tatooine, Ody Mandrell is one of the crowd's favored pilots—young, daring, and with a powerful podracer that causes plenty of damage to other craft in the race. That is, until he pulls over to a pit stop and a pit droid is sucked right through his massive engine. Now he is out of the race!

PLO KOON

JEDI HIGH COUNCIL MEMBER

DATA FILE

AFFILIATION: Jedi
HOMEWORLD: Dorin
SPECIES: Kel Dor
HEIGHT: 1.88m (6ft 2in)
APPEARANCES: I, II, CW, III
SEE ALSO: Qui-Gon Jinn;
Ki-Adi-Mundi

Antiox
mask

Plo Koon's starfighter crashes
into a city on the Neimoidian
planet of Cato Neimoidia.

Thick hide covers body

Loose Jedi cloak

PLO KOON is a member of
the Jedi High Council and
a Jedi General in the Clone
Wars. He is one of the most
powerful Jedi ever, with
awesome fighting abilities
and strong telekinetic
powers. He also discovered
Ahsoka Tano as an infant
and inducted her into
the Jedi Order.

PLO KOON

is a Kel Dor from Dorin. He
wears a special mask to
protect his sensitive eyes
and nostrils from the
oxygen-rich atmosphere
of planets such as
Coruscant. Master Plo
fights in the Battle
of Geonosis and
many more
conflicts in the
Clone Wars.

Tragic Mission

At the end of the Clone Wars,
Plo Koon, an expert pilot, leads
a starfighter patrol above Cato
Neimoidia. Without warning, his own
clone troopers begin firing at his ship.
Order 66 had been given, causing all
the pre-programmed clones to turn on
their Jedi leaders. Plo's ship crashes
into the planet, and Koon is killed.

Practical
combat/flight
boots

ALIEN OUTLAW PILOTS

DATA FILE

HOMEWORLD: Hok (Mawhonic)
SPECIES: Gran (Mawhonic)
HEIGHT: 1.22m (4ft) (Mawhonic)
APPEARANCES: I
SEE ALSO: Sebulba

Three eye stalks

The 18 podracers of Tatooine's famous Boonta Eve Classic line up on the starting grid.

PODRACING IS

not a sport for the faint-hearted! Podracers race at upward of 800 kph (497 mph). No wonder it is a sport suited to the lightning reflexes and body mutations of alien species. In fact, the only unusual sight on the circuit would be a human pilot!

MAWHONIC is a typical podracer from the Outer Rim. He lives outside the laws of the Republic, buying and selling spare parts to Hutts but refusing official Republic currency. His triocular vision comes in handy for split-second timing in races.

Wrist guard

Two stomachs proudly encased in armor plate

Born to Race

Podracer pilots come in all shapes and sizes. Xexto pilots like Gasgano have 24 fingers, which allow them to operate multiple controls at once. Dugs like Sebulba stand on their "arms" (back limbs), while Xamsters like Neva Kee have adapted brains that process sensory data at high speed.

Podracing is an incredibly dangerous sport!

POE DAMERON

DATA FILE

AFFILIATION: Resistance
HOMEWORLD: Yavin 4
SPECIES: Human
HEIGHT: 1.75m (5ft 9in)
APPEARANCES: VII
SEE ALSO: Rey; Finn;
Princess Leia; BB-8

Flight suit

Glie-44 blaster

Positive-grip boots

Poe's astromech droid,
BB-8, serves him well.

AN INCREDIBLY skilled
starfighter pilot, Poe
Dameron is a commander
in the Resistance's fight
against the First Order.
He soars into battle as
Black Leader, behind
the controls of a specially
modified T-70 X-wing.

POE GREW UP
hearing legends of the
fighter pilots of the Rebel
Alliance from his mother,
Shara Bey, who flew an
A-wing during the Battle of
Endor. Poe's father was Kes
Dameron, a Rebel Alliance
Pathfinder soldier.

Joining the Resistance

Poe was raised on Yavin 4, in a colony not far
from the original base of the rebel fighters that
destroyed the first Death Star. Poe's desire to
serve as a pilot landed him as a squadron
leader in the New Republic starfighter forces,
but he defected to the Resistance to bring the
fight directly to the First Order.

POGGLE THE LESSER

GEONOSIAN ARCHDUKE

DATA FILE

AFFILIATION: Separatists
HOMEWORLD: Geonosis
SPECIES: Geonosian
HEIGHT: 1.83m (6ft)
APPEARANCES:
II, CW II
SEE ALSO:
Geonosian
soldier; Count
Dooku

THE ARCHDUKE OF GEONOSIS,
Poggle the Lesser, rules the
Stalgasin hive colony, which controls
all the other major hive colonies
on Geonosis. His factories build
innumerable battle droids for the
Separatists, using the labor of
legions of downtrodden drones.

Long wattles

High-caste wings

Aristocratic adornments

Command staff

POGGLE emerged from
a lower caste through the sheer
force of his iron will to become
Archduke. He is the public face
of the Geonosian aristocracy
and arms business. Hidden
beneath the hives of his planet
is his monarch, Karina the Great,
an enormous Geonosian queen
whose vast egg chambers
propagate the species.

Presiding Leaders

Poggle the Lesser presides over
the first meeting of the Separatist
leadership on his planet, as well
as the trial of Anakin Skywalker,
Obi-Wan Kenobi, and Padmé
Amidala, who are accused of spying.
Poggle and the other Separatists
take refuge in the underlevels
when Republic forces arrive.

Commissioned to design a
superweapon, Poggle hands
the plans to Count Dooku.

POLIS MASSAN

TELEPATHIC KALLIDAHIN

DATA FILE

AFFILIATION: Republic
HOMEWORLD: Kallidah
SPECIES: Kallidahin
HEIGHT: 1.4m (4ft 7in)
APPEARANCES: III
SEE ALSO: Padmé Amidala

Polis Massa is a large rock that was once part of a planet that blew apart in a violent cataclysm.

Remote control

THE PEACEFUL, silent aliens who inhabit Polis Massa are known as Polis Massans, but in fact are Kallidahin from Kallidah. They have become known as Polis Massans because they have spent so long on this rocky planetoid in the Outer Rim.

Sample containers

Diagnostic fingertips

Knee pads

POLIS MASSANS are archaeologists and exobiologists who borrow some of the Kaminoans' cloning techniques to attempt to recreate life from tissues recovered from archaeological digs. They have been excavating Polis Massa, seeking remains of the extinct Eellayin civilization that they believe was ancestor to the Kallidahin.

Urgent Delivery

Yoda and Bail Organa flee to remote Polis Massa to escape Order 66. They are joined by Obi-Wan Kenobi, C-3PO, R2-D2, and Padmé Amidala, who is injured and about to give birth. Polis Massans and medical droids urgently work together to deliver Padmé's twins, Luke and Leia, but they cannot save Padmé herself.

PONDA BABA

AQUALISH THUG

DATA FILE

AFFILIATION: Smuggler
HOMEWORLD: Ando
SPECIES: Aqualish
HEIGHT: 1.7m (5ft 7in)
APPEARANCES: IV
SEE ALSO: Doctor Evazan;
Obi-Wan Kenobi

Large eyes for
seeing underwater
on native planet

PONDA BABA is a thuggish Aqualish who tries to pick a fight with Luke Skywalker. Luke enters a notorious Mos Eisley cantina with Obi-Wan Kenobi looking for a ride off-planet. Ponda Baba's big mistake is picking on the companion of a Jedi.

Stump left by
severing of arm

Facial tusks
grow with age

PONDA BABA met Dr. Evazan when he saved the doctor's life. Together, they shipped spice for Jabba the Hutt. After the fight in the cantina, Evazan tries to use his medical training to reattach Ponda Baba's arm but fails, nearly killing the Aqualish in the process.

Teak Sidbam is a fellow Aqualish who is sometimes mistaken for Ponda Baba.

Cantina Confrontation

Ponda Baba and his partner in crime, Dr. Evazan, are caught unprepared for an old man's ability with a lightsaber (an almost forgotten relic of the glory days of the Galactic Republic). But for Luke, too, this first demonstration of Kenobi's abilities with the weapon is a revelation, and a hint of the possible return of the Jedi.

POWER DROID

DATA FILE

AFFILIATION: None
TYPE: Power droid
MANUFACTURER:
Industrial Automaton
and Veril Line Systems
APPROX. HEIGHT:
1m (3ft 3in)
APPEARANCES: I, CW,
R, IV, V, VI, VII
SEE ALSO: 2-1B;
C-3PO

SOME DROIDS ARE made for greatness, like sophisticated pilot or surgeon droids; others, like C-3PO, have greatness thrust upon them. But some droids are so commonplace, they are destined never to be noticed. Power droids, which function as mobile power generators, are such droids.

Power plugs

Monochromatic photoreceptor

Power droids have very simple artificial intelligence, so they tend to get lost easily.

Internal power generator

POWER DROIDS, either
the EG-series, made by Veril Line Systems, or the GNK-series, made by Industrial Automaton, are sometimes named "gonk" droids because of the low honking noise they emit. Industrial Automaton also made a tibanna gas-holding PLNK-series power droid in the Clone Wars.

GNK Power Droids
In less-developed backwaters all around the galaxy, wherever there is a junk shop or a mechanic garage, it is likely there will be GNK power droids somewhere in the background. Watto's junk shop on Tatooine has a few battered GNK units. Watto gives run-down merchandise a quick power-up to get a better price from customers.

PRINCESS LEIA

GENERAL OF THE RESISTANCE

DATA FILE

AFFILIATION: Rebel Alliance/
Resistance
HOMEWORLD: Alderaan
SPECIES: Human
HEIGHT: 1.55m (5ft 1in)
APPEARANCES: III, IV, V, VI, VII
SEE ALSO: Bail Organa;
Luke Skywalker; Han Solo

AS SENATOR for Alderaan, Princess Leia Organa made diplomatic missions across the galaxy on her ship, the *Tantive IV*. Secretly, Leia worked for the Rebel Alliance, and she played a vital role in the defeat of the Empire.

Resistance
uniform

RAISED ON Alderaan by her adoptive father, Bail Organa, Leia was well prepared for her royal position, and used her high-placed connections wherever she could to aid the Alliance. During the decades of peace that follow the destruction of the Empire, Leia is able to concentrate on her new family, but as the galaxy once again undergoes turmoil, she returns to her role as a military commander.

Decisive Leader

Leia was a key command figure in the Rebel Alliance, overseeing important missions and planning strategy, alongside General Rieekan and other Alliance leaders. In Echo Base on Hoth, Leia peered intently at the scanners, alert to any signs of Imperial detection.

Leia commands the Resistance from its hidden base on the planet D'Qar.

Travel boots

PZ-4CO

COMMUNICATIONS DROID

DATA FILE

AFFILIATION: Resistance
TYPE: Communications droid
MANUFACTURER: Serv-O-Droid
HEIGHT: 2.06m (6ft 9in)
APPEARANCES: VII
SEE ALSO: Princess Leia; Admiral Statura; C-3PO; Snap Wexley

Elongated neck

Data storage center

Intermotor actuating coupler

Fine manipulators

A CONSTANT FIXTURE in the Resistance base control rooms, PZ-4CO offers tactical data and communications support during important operations. She speaks in a pleasant, female voice.

THE PREVALENCE

of humanoid species in the galaxy has helped shape the forms of most protocol droids, as they are designed to mimic the life forms they interact with. PZ-4CO's anatomy is specifically modeled on the long-necked Tofallid species.

Intelligence Droids

PZ-4CO is one of many droids that form an invisible Resistance intelligence network. Droid agents scattered across the galaxy transmit reports back to Resistance headquarters, which PZ-4CO and C-3PO then assess in order to paint a real-time picture of First Order movements.

QUEEN APAILANA

PADMÉ AMIDALA'S SUCCESSOR

DATA FILE

AFFILIATION: Republic
HOMEWORLD: Naboo
SPECIES: Human
HEIGHT: 1.57m (5ft 2in)
APPEARANCES: III
SEE ALSO: Padmé Amidala

Fan headdress worn in tribute to Padmé Amidala

THOUGH YOUNG, Queen Apailana has the qualities that the Naboo look for in their rulers: purity of heart and an absolute dedication to the peaceful values of the planet.

White makeup is ancient Naboo royal custom

Veda pearl suspensas

Cerlin capelet

QUEEN APAILANA

is elected Queen of Naboo when she is just 12 years old. One of the youngest monarchs in the planet's history, she begins her reign towards the end of the Clone Wars.

Chersilk mourning robe

Thousands follow Padmé Amidala's funeral procession through Theed.

Standing Strong

Queen Apailana is one of the chief mourners at Padmé Amidala's funeral on Naboo. Padmé had supported Apailana's bid for election. Although the official explanation for Padmé's death is that she died at the hands of renegade Jedi, Apailana privately believes otherwise.

QUI-GON JINN

DATA FILE

AFFILIATION: Jedi
HOMEWORLD: Coruscant
SPECIES: Human
HEIGHT: 1.93m (6ft 4in)
APPEARANCES: I, II, CW
SEE ALSO: Anakin Skywalker

Qui-Gon Jinn is one of the few Jedi to have battled a Sith—Darth Maul.

Long hair worn back to keep vision clear

Jinn's dying wish is that Obi-Wan trains Anakin.

QUI-GON JINN

is an experienced but headstrong Jedi Master. He was Padawan to Count Dooku and teacher to Obi-Wan Kenobi. Jinn has sometimes clashed with the Jedi High Council over his favoring of risk and action: as a result, he has not been offered a seat on the Council.

Jedi tunic

The Chosen One

When Jinn encounters young Anakin Skywalker, he believes he has discovered the prophesied individual who will bring balance to the Force. Jinn makes a bet with slave owner Watto: if the boy wins his podrace, then he also wins his freedom. If he loses, Jinn loses his ship. The risk pays off, and Jinn takes the boy to Coruscant to present him to the Jedi High Council, with mixed results.

QUI-GON JINN

fights actively for the Galactic Republic, but he is struck down by the unruly dark energies of Darth Maul. After his death, Jinn becomes the first Jedi to live on in the Force, a gift he will pass on to Obi-Wan Kenobi, Yoda, and Anakin Skywalker.

Rugged travel boots

R2-D2

THE BRAVEST DROID IN THE GALAXY

DATA FILE

AFFILIATION: Republic/ Rebel Alliance/Resistance
TYPE: R-2 series astromech droid
MANUFACTURER: Industrial Automaton
HEIGHT: 1.09m (3ft 7in)
APPEARANCES: I, II, CW, III, R, IV, V, VI, VII
SEE ALSO: C-3PO; Princess Leia; Bail Organa

R2-D2 IS NO ORDINARY astromech droid. His long history of adventures has given him a distinct personality. He is stubborn and inventive, and is strongly motivated to succeed at any given task. Although R2-D2 speaks only in electronic beeps and whistles, he usually manages to make his point!

Holographic projector

R2-D2 has many hidden tricks, including extension arms and rocket boosters.

R2-D2 first distinguishes himself on board Queen Amidala's Royal Starship. He serves Anakin Skywalker during the Clone Wars and then Luke Skywalker during the Rebellion, flying in the droid socket of their spaceships.

Powerbus cables

Motorized, all-terrain treads

Risky Mission

At the end of the Clone Wars, R2-D2 is assigned to Bail Organa's diplomatic fleet. Princess Leia entrusts R2-D2 with the stolen Death Star plans and her urgent message to Obi-Wan Kenobi. He risks all kinds of damage to accomplish his mission.

R4-G9

DATA FILE

AFFILIATION: Republic
TYPE: Astromech droid
MANUFACTURER: Industrial
Automaton
HEIGHT: 96cm (3ft 2in)
APPEARANCES: III
SEE ALSO: Obi-Wan
Kenobi; R4-P17

R4-G9 IS a bronze-domed astromech droid that is stationed at the Jedi Temple on Coruscant. She is briefly assigned to Obi-Wan Kenobi when he begins flying a new class of starfighter, while his regular droid, R4-P17, is being adapted to fit the new ship. Kenobi uses R4-G9 again on his crucial mission to Utapau.

One of R4-G9's tasks is to transmit coordinates to the starfighter's hyperspace docking ring.

Reader socket
for data cards

Primary system
ventilation port

Tactics

Kenobi uses R4-G9 on Utapau after his own R4-P17 unit is destroyed in the Battle of Coruscant. In a diversionary tactic, R4-G9 pilots Kenobi's ship off the planet alone and returns to the Star Destroyer *Vigilance*, while Obi-Wan remains to track down General Grievous.

R4-G9 was first assigned to Aayla Secura on her starfighter. Secura once loaned Kenobi her ship and droid during a search for Asajj Ventress. Kenobi took the precaution of having R4-P17 upload his flight history records to R4-G9.

High-power
coupling for
system recharge

Power cables for
mobility control

Housing holds
main drive motor

164

R4-P17

OBI-WAN KENOBI'S ASTROMECH DROID

DATA FILE

AFFILIATION: Republic
TYPE: Astromech droid
MANUFACTURER: Industrial Automaton
HEIGHT: 96cm (3ft 2in)
APPEARANCES: II, CW, III
SEE ALSO: Obi-Wan Kenobi

R4-P17 IS Obi-Wan Kenobi's trusty astromech droid, used in his red starfighter. Before the Clone Wars, she was copilot when Kenobi chased Jango Fett through the asteroid rings above Geonosis. R4-P17 continued to assist Obi-Wan during the Clone Wars and participated in the Battle of Teth among others.

R4-P17 compensates for Obi-Wan's dislike of flying by taking over most tasks, though he often asks her not to try any fancy maneuvers.

Onboard logic function displays

A buzz droid slices off R4-P17's domed head in the Battle of Coruscant.

Panels conceal tools

Standardized arm

Treaded drives

Repurposed

Before the Clone Wars, R4-P17 had a specially modified body, which fitted into the narrow wing of Kenobi's starfighter. She was later repurposed and now has a full astromech body so she can fit into the latest models of starfighters.

R5-D4

ASTROMECH DROID SET TO DESTRUCT

DATA FILE

AFFILIATION: Rebel Alliance
TYPE: Astromech droid
MANUFACTURER: Industrial
Automaton
HEIGHT: 97cm (3ft 2in)
APPEARANCES: II, IV
SEE ALSO: R2-D2;
Owen Lars; Jawa

R5-D4, ALSO KNOWN as "Red," is a white and red astromech droid that Jawas on Tatooine sell to Owen Lars. However, immediately after the sale, Red's motivator blows up, and Owen returns him to the Jawas. This gives C-3PO the opportunity he needs to recommend that Owen takes R2-D2 instead.

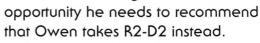

Photoreceptor

Jawas hastily retrieve the inert R5-D4 from their disgusted customer.

R5-D4 belongs to a series of droids that are cut-price versions of the superior R2 units. They are prone to defects and bad attitudes.

Panel conceals systems linkage and repair arms

Recharge coupling

Sabotage

What Owen and Luke do not know is that R2-D2 sabotaged R5-D4 when they were inside the Jawas' sandcrawler. Usually, droids' programming forbids them to mess with other droids, but Leia has instructed R2 to complete his mission at any cost.

Third tread for balance over uneven surfaces

RANCOR

JABBA'S RAVENOUS PET

DATA FILE

HOMEWORLD: Dathomir
HEIGHT: 5–19m
(16ft 5in–62ft 4in)
DIET: Carnivorous
APPEARANCES: CW, VI
SEE ALSO: Jabba the Hutt;
Bib Fortuna; Malakili

FEARSOME RANCOR MONSTERS are more than five meters (16 feet) tall, with thick skin and enormous strength. One specimen lives in a pit below Jabba the Hutt's throne room. The slimy, depraved gangster likes nothing more than to watch the rancor attack any unfortunate victims he chooses to cast into the pit.

Weak eyesight

Armored skin can deflect laser bolts

Razor-sharp teeth

Luke Skywalker prepares to battle for his life in Jabba's rancor pit.

Hungry Beast

Jabba can operate a secret trap door located in front of his throne, which leads directly to his pet rancor below. When Luke Skywalker is thrown down, a Gamorrean guard falls with him and is then crushed in the rancor's jaws.

RANCORS come from a remote planet named Dathomir. Most people think that rancors are entirely savage but in fact they have a primitive intelligence. Jabba's major-domo, Bib Fortuna, presented a rancor to Jabba as a birthday gift.

RAPPERTUNIE

MAX REBO BAND MEMBER

DATA FILE

AFFILIATION: Jabba's court
HOMEWORLD: Manpha
SPECIES: Shawda Ubb
HEIGHT: 30cm (12in)
APPEARANCES: VI
SEE ALSO: Max Rebo

RAPPERTUNIE plays a combination flute, or Growdi Harmonique, in Max Rebo's Band. Rappertunie has always had a thirst for travel and has used his musical talent to pay his way around the galaxy. Unfortunately, he ends up in a lifetime gig at Jabba's palace, where the hot, dry climate does not suit his moist skin at all.

Defense

At Jabba's palace, Rappertunie can spend whole days perched motionless on his Growdi seat, trying to keep his naturally moist skin cool. Being small in size makes Rappertunie feel quite vulnerable, but he can spit paralyzing poison at those who threaten him.

RAPPERTUNIE

is a Shawda-Ubb—a small, amphibious species with long fingers. Rappertunie was born on the swampy, wet Outer Rim planet, Manpha.

Naturally moist skin

Three fingers adapted for amphibious life on home planet

Growdi

Rappertunie plays away at the rear of the stage while secretly plotting his escape.

RATHTAR

NIGHTMARE MONSTER

DATA FILE

HOMEWORLD: Unknown
HEIGHT: 1.68m (5ft 6in)
DIET: Carnivorous
HABITAT: Jungle
APPEARANCES: VII
SEE ALSO: Han Solo; Chewbacca

THE ENORMOUS tentacled beasts responsible for such disasters as the Trillia Massacre, rathtars are universally terrifying. Even so, their intimidating presence, unique biology, and exotic rarity mean there is a demand for these creatures on the black market.

Solo's Gamble

King Prana offers a big bounty to anyone who can deliver him a live rathtar for his menagerie. Han Solo takes on the assignment, hauling rathtars inside his massive freighter, the *Eravana*. The creatures break loose from their cages while Solo is surrounded by gangsters, transforming a tense standoff into a deadly eruption of chaos.

RATHARS HAVE

traits that suggest they are evolutionarily primitive: rudimentary light-sensing "eyes," a lack of a true skeleton, and reproduction through fission. Despite this their hunting methods can, at times, seem extremely sophisticated.

Radial mouth

Muscular tentacles

Club-like terminus

RAZOO QIN-FEE

KANJIKLUB GANGSTER

A LIEUTENANT in the cutthroat Kanjiklub gang, Razoo Qin-Fee specializes in weapons maintenance and modification. The bandits of Kanjiklub favor crude and deadly weaponry and explosives. Qin-Fee upgrades and modifies them to dangerous specifications.

Homemade explosive cylinders

Spare blaster gas ammunition cartridge

AUTHORITY IN

Kanjiklub is a violent affair—as is everything in this Outer Rim gang. Razoo Qin-Fee eyes the role of leader, currently held by Tasu Leech. However, he must make enough allies first, so that he is not instantly overthrown by others in the gang.

Razoo Qin-Fee accompanies Tasu Leech while boarding Han Solo's freighter, the *Eravana*, in an ill-fated attempt to collect money that Solo owes Kanjiklub.

Lethal Lieutenant

Razoo Qin-Fee earned a dangerous reputation in the underworld Zygerrian fighting circuit, where he was banned for exceptionally dirty tactics. Though he is a fierce unarmed warrior, he is also a pyromaniac and tech expert. His extensively modified blaster rifle, which he has named the "Wasp," packs a powerful sting.

REBEL TROOPER

DATA FILE

AFFILIATION: Rebel Alliance
SPECIES: Human
STANDARD EQUIPMENT:
Blaster pistol
APPEARANCES: IV, V, VI
SEE ALSO: General Madine

Lightweight combat helmet

REBEL SOLDIERS are the main forces of the Alliance to Restore the Republic. These dedicated troops are organized into Sector Forces, each of which is responsible for resisting the might of the Empire in their home sectors across the galaxy.

Fleet troopers on the *Tantive IV* wear a uniform of blue shirts, black combat vests, and gray pants.

High-resistance gloves

Commandos

Alliance SpecForce wilderness fighters infiltrate an Imperial base on Endor's forest moon. Under the command of General Solo, they manage to trick the squadrons of Imperial troops inside the base to come out, where they are outnumbered and forced to surrender.

REBEL TROOPS wear

standardized uniforms wherever the Alliance's meager resources allow. SpecForce wilderness fighters—soldiers trained for specialized roles in Alliance Special Forces—wear full forest-camouflaged fatigues during the Battle of Endor.

Camouflaged cargo pants

Heavy-duty boots

REEK

GEONOSIAN ARENA BEASTS

DATA FILE

HOMEWORLD: Ylesia, Codian Moon
HEIGHT: 2m (6ft 7in) high, 4m (13ft 1in) long
DIET: Omnivorous
HABITAT: Grasslands
APPEARANCES: II, CW
SEE ALSO: Nexu; acklay

IN THE BRUTAL AND bloody arenas on Geonosis, reeks are one of the ferocious species kept for the purposes of execution and sport. Up against one of these mighty beasts, Anakin Skywalker manages to use his Force powers to tame the reek enough to ride it, rather than letting it kill him.

Combat

Reeks are slow-moving and heavy. However, they are dangerous fighters, with powerful jaws and horns that can gore opponents. In the wild, these horns are used for combat with other reeks.

Anakin gets the better of the arena reek, which Jango Fett later kills.

Red coloration produced by unnatural meat diet

Horn-teeth grow continuously

Sprawling posture makes reek relatively slow-moving

Cheek horns for dominance-combat headlocks

REEKS ARE naturally herbivores. The Geonosians starve them into eating meat to increase their aggression and provide entertainment in the arenas.

REY

JAKKU SCAVENGER

DATA FILE

AFFILIATION: Resistance
HOMEWORLD: Jakku
SPECIES: Human
HEIGHT: 1.7m (5ft 7in)
APPEARANCES: VII
SEE ALSO: Finn; BB-8;
Han Solo; Luke Skywalker

A 19-YEAR-OLD scavenger who lives in the inhospitable deserts of Jakku, Rey never intends to leave the desolate planet. She holds out hope that those who left her there will someday return.

Tight bindings

Salvaged quarterstaff

DESPITE A HARD life that should have left her free of sympathy and compassion, Rey takes pity on a stranded little droid named BB-8. Rather than trade the valuable Resistance droid for food, she keeps watch over it.

Rey is surprised to learn that she has a vital role to play in the fate of the galaxy, and perhaps the Force itself.

Heroes of the Past

Rey's life is catapulted into a galactic adventure when her path collides with Finn, a deserter from the First Order. The two join forces to get BB-8 back into the hands of the Resistance, and flee Jakku aboard the commandeered *Millennium Falcon*. This brings Rey face-to-face with Han Solo, the first of several legendary heroes of the Galactic Civil War that she will meet.

RYSTÁLL

PERFORMER IN THE MAX REBO BAND

DATA FILE

AFFILIATION: Jabba's court
HOMEWORLD: Coruscant
SPECIES: Half Theelin/
half human
HEIGHT: 1.7m (5ft 7in)
APPEARANCES: III, VI
SEE ALSO: Greeata; Lyn Me

RYSTÁLL SANT'S adoptive parents are Ortolan musicians from Coruscant. They arrange for their dazzling daughter to perform as a singer and dancer with Max Rebo's band, where she will turn heads.

Rystáll and fellow singer Greeata are shocked by the depravities they witness at Jabba's palace.

Natural markings highlighted with stage makeup

RYSTÁLL IS part human and part Theelin. The Theelin are a rare species with head horns, brightly colored hair, and mottled skin. Rystáll also has hooved feet. Many Theelin have artistic personalities and choose to become artists or performers.

Cape is a gift from a passing admirer, Syrh Rhoams

Dancer's graceful body

Hooves

Star Attraction

The colorful Rystáll Sant has always attracted the attention of a variety of characters, including the high-placed lieutenant in the criminal Black Sun organization, who tricked her into slavery. Lando Calrissian later freed her. At Jabba's palace she attracts the attention of bounty hunter Boba Fett.

SABÉ

ROYAL NABOO HANDMAIDEN

Royal headdress

Scar of remembrance

DATA FILE

AFFILIATION: Royal House of Naboo
HOMEWORLD: Naboo
SPECIES: Human
HEIGHT: 1.65m (5ft 5in)
APPEARANCES: 1
SEE ALSO: Padmé Amidala

SABÉ IS THE MOST

important handmaiden in Queen Amidala's entourage. She is first in line to become the royal decoy in times of danger. Sabé dresses as the Queen and disguises her features with white makeup.

Surcoat

Broad waistband

QUEEN AMIDALA'S

handmaidens assist with many tasks necessary to maintain the monarch's regal image. These capable individuals are also trained in bodyguard skills and are equipped with blaster pistols to defend their monarch in the event of a disturbance or emergency.

Long battle-dress made of blast-damping fabric

Sabé leads the delegation to ask the Gungans to join the Naboo in the fight for their planet.

Royal Service

While Sabé is disguised as the Queen, Padmé Amidala dresses in the simple gown of a handmaiden. They use silent gestures and expressions to communicate secretly with each other. Sabé is trained to imitate the Queen in every way, but the task is a risky one.

SAESEE TIIN

IKTOTCHI JEDI MASTER

SAESEE

DATA FILE

AFFILIATION: Jedi
HOMEWORLD: Iktotch
SPECIES: Iktotchi
HEIGHT: 1.88m (6ft 2in)
APPEARANCES: I, II, CW, III
SEE ALSO: Mace Windu

JEDI MASTER SAESEE TIIN sits on the High Council in the Jedi Temple on Coruscant. He is particularly skilled in piloting the finest spacecraft at high speeds, which is also when his telepathic mind does its most focused thinking.

Well-developed horns

Lightsaber

Customary humanoid Jedi robes

Tough skin protects against high winds of Iktotchon

SAESEE TIIN was born on Iktotch, the moon of Iktotchon. He is a natural pilot, exhibiting an instinctive sense of direction and a fine control of ships of many different sizes. During an important Clone Wars mission to Lola Sayu, the site of the Separatist Citadel installation, Tiin pilots his well maintained starfighter into battle.

Jedi Fighter

Saesee Tiin fights at the Battle of Geonosis, riding on a Republic gunship to attack the droids on the plains. Later in the battle, Tiin takes to the skies to aid Jedi Master Adi Gallia in the battle above Geonosis. Tiin becomes a General in the Clone Wars, leading starfighter squadrons.

Tiin is one of the Jedi who confront Palpatine, now revealed to be Sidious.

SALACIOUS CRUMB

KOWAKIAN MONKEY-LIZARD

DATA FILE

AFFILIATION: Jabba's court
HOMEWORLD: Kowak
SPECIES: Kowakian
Monkey-Lizard
HEIGHT: 70cm (2ft 4in)
APPEARANCES: VI
SEE ALSO: Jabba the Hutt

SALACIOUS CRUMB is Jabba the Hutt's court jester. When Jabba first found this Kowakian Monkey-Lizard stealing his food, the Hutt tried to eat him. Crumb escaped but Bib Fortuna captured him.

Highly sensitive ears

Hooked reptilian beak

Collar of scruffy fur

Spindly arm

Crumb often irritates guests by repeating whatever Jabba says.

In Jest

Salacious Crumb knows that he must make Jabba laugh at least once a day, otherwise he will be killed. Crumb picks on everyone around him to entertain his boss, especially Jabba's new translator droid, C-3PO, who loses an eye to the hateful little creature.

SALACIOUS CRUMB

was just one of the many vermin on a space station, until he managed to stow away on board one of Jabba's spaceships, ending up on Tatooine. Now Crumb sits beside Jabba the Hutt, teasing all the inhabitants of the palace.

Sharp talons

SANDTROOPER

DESERT-READY STORMTROOPERS

DATA FILE

AFFILIATION: Empire
SPECIES: Human
HEIGHT: 1.83m (6ft)
STANDARD EQUIPMENT:
Blaster pistol; blaster rifle;
repeating blaster
APPEARANCES: IV
SEE ALSO: Stormtrooper

SANDTROOPERS are specialized Imperial stormtroopers, trained to adapt to desert environments. They are equipped with armor and weapons for use in hot, dry climates. Their armor uses advanced cooling systems and their helmets have built-in polarized lenses to reduce sun glare.

Anti-sun glare lenses

Comlink system

Pauldron indicates rank

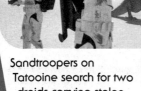

Sandtroopers on Tatooine search for two droids carrying stolen Death Star plans.

Utility belt

SANDTROOPERS

are human recruits who remain anonymous behind their white armor. They carry food and water supplies, blaster rifles, and long-range comlinks. Sandtroopers' training enables them to adapt to local customs, like riding native dewback lizards on Tatooine.

Ranks

Sandtroopers wear shoulder pauldrons, which indicate rank. Regular sandtroopers' pauldrons are black, while sergeants wear white pauldrons. Squad leaders, who lead units of seven troopers, wear orange pauldrons.

SARCO PLANK

GALACTIC OUTLAW

DATA FILE

AFFILIATION: None
HOMEWORLD: Unknown
SPECIES: Melitto
HEIGHT: 1.82m (6ft)
APPEARANCES: VII
SEE ALSO: Luke Skywalker;
C-3PO; Unkar Plutt; Rey

A SCAVENGER and bounty hunter, the sinister Sarco Plank works as an arms trader at Niima Outpost on Jakku, where he sells weapons to explorers willing to brave the desert wastes in search of valuable salvage.

DURING the Galactic Civil War, Sarco worked as a tomb raider, robbing ancient sites such as the Temple of Eedit, a Jedi outpost on Devaron. In that expedition, Sarco lured a young Luke Skywalker to the temple, hoping the youth could unlock the site's secrets. Sarco fought Luke, wielding an electrostaff against Skywalker's lightsaber, but failed to defeat the rebel pilot.

Vocoder helmet

Nutrient and fluid dispenser

Eyeless Alien

Sarco Plank lacks eyes—his face is a featureless wall of insectoid plates. He senses his surroundings based on vibrations transmitted by ultra-sensitive hairs known as cilia, which line his body. A vocoder built into his feeding mask translates the humming of his face plates into an understandable voice.

SARLACC

LETHAL SAND-DWELLING LIFE-FORMS

DATA FILE

HOMEWORLD: Tatooine
WIDTH: 3m (9ft 10in)
DIET: Omnivorous
HABITAT: Desert
APPEARANCES: VI
SEE ALSO: Boba Fett

IT IS FORTUNATE THAT the sarlaccs are so rare in the galaxy, since they are so utterly unpleasant. These monstrous life-forms hide beneath desert sands with their mouths just below the surface. Unwary individuals can easily find themselves slipping beneath the dunes into the waiting jaws of the terrifying creature.

Inward-pointing teeth prevent victims from escaping

Touch-receptor tentacles

THE MONSTROUS

Sarlacc, which rests in the basin of the Great Pit of Carkoon in the Northern Dune Sea on Tatooine, is a favorite means for Jabba to dispose of any individuals who have particularly displeased him.

Captured Prey

Jabba intends to watch the Sarlacc feasting on Luke Skywalker and his friends. While the rebels manage to escape its jaws and make a daring escape, others are not so lucky. The creature feasts on many bodies that day. Kithaba, one of Jabba's slaves, is one unlucky victim.

The beaked tongue that rises from the Sarlacc's toothed mouth can swallow prey whole.

SCOUT TROOPER

SPECIALIZED STORMTROOPERS

IMPERIAL SCOUT TROOPERS
are trained for long-term missions.
They wear armor on the head
and upper body only, to allow
maximum maneuverability.
Their helmets have enhanced
macrobinocular viewplates,
for precision target
identification.

Survival rations

SCOUT TROOPERS

are sent to survey areas and
locate enemy positions, infiltrate
enemy territory, and undertake
sabotage missions. They rarely
engage in combat, and are
instructed to call in stormtroopers
at any signs of trouble.

Body glove

The Republic first
deployed clone scout
troopers during the Clone
Wars, including the Battle
of Kachirho on Kashyyyk.

Pistol holder

On Patrol

Scout troopers on speeder bikes
patrol the dense forests of Endor,
where the Empire maintains a
strategic shield generator. Working
in units of two or four, they watch
for any signs of troublesome forest
creatures or terrorist infiltrators.

SEBULBA

STAR PODRACER

SEBULBA IS ONE of the top podracers in the Outer Rim circuits. He is skilled at piloting his vehicle, but also willing to use dirty tricks to give him the winning edge. When Anakin Skywalker joins a race, Sebulba decides the young human must not win.

DATA FILE

AFFILIATON: None
HOMEWORLD: Malastare
SPECIES: Dug
HEIGHT: 1.12m (3ft 8in)
APPEARANCES: I
SEE ALSO: Podracers

Grasping hands

Race goggles

SEBULBA

is a Dug from Malastare, a species notorious for being bullies. Playing up to his tough, violent image for the crowds, Sebulba wears a flashy, custom-designed leather racing suit.

Beaded danglers

Sebulba pilots a giant, orange podracer with many secret weapons concealed in it.

Leather wrist guard

Dangerous Driver

The dastardly Dug gives himself the winning edge in races by sabotaging other racers. Sebulba can pull up alongside another podracer and blast it with his hidden flame thrower, or throw concussion weapons into another pilot's cockpit.

Trophy coins

Although Sebulba crashes during the Boonta Eve Classic, he survives to race in other competitions.

Tight leather leg-straps

SECURITY DROID

ARMED BATTLE DROIDS

DATA FILE

AFFILIATON: Separatists
TYPE: Battle droid
MANUFACTURER: Baktoid
Combat Automata
HEIGHT: 1.91m (6ft 3in)
APPEARANCES: I, II, CW, III
SEE ALSO: Battle droid

Optical sensor

Droid type designation markings

Arm extension piston

High-torque motors

Security droids on board *Invisible Hand* are about to become scrap metal.

E-5 blaster rifle

SECURITY DROIDS WITH red markings are programmed for defense on spaceships, space stations, or buildings. These specialized droids work in squads led by a command officer battle droid with yellow markings.

Droid Assault

Security droids patrol many Trade Federation capital ships. At the start of the blockade of Naboo, Jedi Qui-Gon Jinn and Obi-Wan Kenobi board the Trade Federation flagship to begin negotiations, and instead have to defend themselves from security droids. During the Clone Wars, Anakin and Obi-Wan face many security droids when they rescue Chancellor Palpatine from General Grievous's flagship, *Invisible Hand*.

SECURITY DROIDS use standard E-5 blaster rifles. However, their programming is only a little more complex than regular battle droids, so they frequently miss their targets.

SHAAK TI

TOGRUTA JEDI MASTER

DATA FILE

AFFILIATION: Jedi
HOMEWORLD: Shili
SPECIES: Togruta
HEIGHT: 1.78m (5ft 10in)
APPEARANCES: II, CW, III
SEE ALSO: Luminara Unduli

Characteristic pigmentation of the Togruta species

JEDI MASTER SHAAK TI joined the Jedi High Council before the arena battle on Geonosis. During the Clone Wars, she often represents the Jedi Order on Kamino. Her compassion for the clone troopers as individuals clashes with the Kaminoan scientists' cold view that they are products.

Hollow montrals sense space

Two-handed grip for control

Jedi robe

Shaak Ti is the same species as Anakin Skywalker's apprentice, Ahsoka Tano.

Master Jedi

Ti fights alongside the other 200 Jedi Knights that come to the aid of Anakin Skywalker, Obi-Wan Kenobi, and Padmé Amidala on Geonosis. After the conflict in the arena, she boards a Republic gunship for the front lines of the battle against the massed droid army.

TOGRUTA Shaak Ti is one of the best Jedi fighters in group combat. Her hollow head montrals sense space ultrasonically, sharpening her spatial awareness. Where others struggle with the complexity of movements, Shaak Ti darts with ease.

SHMI SKYWALKER

ANAKIN SKYWALKER'S MOTHER

DATA FILE

AFFILIATION: Slave/moisture farmer
HOMEWORLD: Tatooine
SPECIES: Human
HEIGHT: 1.73m (5ft 8in)
APPEARANCES: I, II, CW
SEE ALSO: Cliegg Lars; Anakin Skywalker; Watto

Simple hairstyle typical of servants

SHMI SKYWALKER HAS lived a hard life as a slave since pirates captured her parents when she was a girl. Owned by junk dealer Watto on Tatooine, Shmi gives birth to a child named Anakin, who also works as a slave.

Decorative belt

IN SPITE OF her poverty, Shmi tries to give Anakin a good home in the slave quarter of Mos Espa. Anakin's departure is hard for Shmi to bear, but she comes to live a happier life when a settler farmer, Cliegg Lars, frees her in order to marry her.

Rough-spun tunic withstands harsh Tatooine weather

Shmi refuses to let her love for Anakin keep him from what she feels is his destiny—to be a Jedi.

Tragic Loss

When Anakin Skywalker senses that his mother is in terrible pain, he travels to Tatooine to help her. However, he cannot prevent her death at the hands of the Sand People. Experiencing great anger and pain, Anakin vows to build his power until nothing can withstand it.

Simple skirt

SHOCK TROOPER

MEMBERS OF THE CORUSCANT GUARD

DATA FILE

AFFILIATION:
Republic/Empire
HOMEWORLD: Kamino
SPECIES: Human clone
HEIGHT: 1.83m (6ft)
APPEARANCES: II, CW, III
SEE ALSO: Stormtrooper

AS THE REPUBLIC PREPARES for war, red-emblazoned shock troopers begin to patrol public spaces on Coruscant, to ensure public order and security. They also serve as bodyguards for politicians, including Supreme Chancellor Palpatine.

Upgraded breath
filter and annunciator

Coruscant
designation

Shock-absorbing
plastoid armor

D15-rifle

In the last days of the Republic, people begin to refer to shock troopers as stormtroopers.

SHOCK TROOPERS

are members of the Coruscant Guard. Palpatine set up the unit to strengthen the Coruscant Security Force and the Senate Guard. Shock troopers keep watch on government buildings and landing platforms.

Palpatine's Guard

Shock troopers go with Palpatine to the Senate after the Jedi's failed attempt to arrest him. After Yoda's battle with Palpatine, they unsuccessfully search for the Jedi Master's body. Shock troopers also accompany Palpatine to Mustafar, where they find Darth Vader's burned body.

SHU MAI

PRESENT OF THE COMMERCE GUILD

DATA FILE

AFFILIATION: Commerce Guild, Separatists
HOMEWORLD: Castell
SPECIES: Gossam
HEIGHT: 1.65m (5ft 5in)
APPEARANCES: II, III
SEE ALSO: Nute Gunray; Wat Tambor; Count Dooku

Shu Mai awaits her fate on volcanic Mustafar with the rest of the Separatist leaders.

Neck rings

Emblazoned jewel crest

SHU MAI IS PRESIDENT of the powerful Commerce Guild, whose forces fight the Republic during the Clone Wars. Mai is a member of the Separatist Council alongside Nute Gunray, Wat Tambor, and others. She is obsessed with status and power.

Rich skirt made of rare uris silk

SHU MAI is a Gossam from the planet Castell. She is only concerned with status, power, and wealth. Mai worked her way up the Commerce Guild using aggressive and unscrupulous tactics, until no rivals stood in her way to becoming President.

Gossams have three-toed feet

Sneaky Practices

Shu Mai is not the only Separatist leader to pledge her support to Dooku in secret, knowing that it amounts to treason. Though the Commerce Guild does not openly back the Separatists, Shu Mai's homing spider droids begin to fight on the battlefields of the Clone Wars.

SIO BIBBLE

GOVERNOR OF NABOO

DATA FILE

AFFILIATION: Royal House of Naboo
HOMEWORLD: Naboo
SPECIES: Human
HEIGHT: 1.7m (5ft 7in)
APPEARANCES: I, II, CW, III
SEE ALSO: Captain Panaka; Nute Gunray; Padmé Amidala

Formal collar

SIO BIBBLE is Governor of Naboo during the Trade Federation invasion. He oversees all matters brought to Queen Amidala's attention. He also chairs the Advisory Council, the governing body of Naboo. Sio is completely opposed to violence.

Fashionable Naboo sleeves and cuffs

Philosopher's tunic

BIBBLE IS A

philosopher who was elected governor under Amidala's predecessor, King Veruna. Sio is initially critical of Amidala, but comes to respect her. He later serves under Amidala's successors Queens Jamillia, Neeyutnee, and Apailana.

Bibble refuses to accept Captain Panaka's warnings of greater need for armament.

Under Arrest

During the invasion of Naboo, battle droids arrest Sio Bibble and Queen Amidala. When two Jedi Knights rescue Amidala, the governor chooses to stay with his people. Bibble leads them in a hunger strike, and earns the ire of the Trade Federation Viceroy, Nute Gunray.

Governor's boots

SLY MOORE

PALPATINE'S STAFF AIDE

Eyes see only in
ultraviolet light

SLY MOORE is Palpatine's Staff
Aide. She wields huge power
because she controls access
to the Chancellor. Moore is
one of the few individuals
who knows that Palpatine's
secret identity is Darth Sidious.

Umbarans conceal
their emotions

Sly Moore often attends
Palpatine's meetings,
silently shadowing the
Supreme Chancellor.

SLY MOORE is an
Umbaran—a technologically
advanced species from
Umbara. This planet is
known as "the Shadow World"
because so little natural light
reaches its surface. Umbarans
are known for their ability to
use their minds to subtly
influence, and control, others.

Power Play

In Palpatine's administration,
Sly Moore holds the post that
Sei Taria had in Chancellor
Valorum's time. Some whisper
that Moore must have
threatened the committed
and dedicated Sei Taria with
blackmail to persuade her
to stand down.

Umbaran shadow cloak is
patterned in ultraviolet colors

SNAP WEXLEY

RESISTANCE RECON PILOT

DATA FILE

AFFILIATION: Resistance
HOMEWORLD: Akiva
SPECIES: Human
HEIGHT: 1.88m (6ft 2in)
APPEARANCES: VII
SEE ALSO: Ello Asty; Princess Leia; Poe Dameron; Jess Pava

A SKILLED X-wing pilot serving in Blue Squadron, Temmin "Snap" Wexley is a captain in the Resistance, and recognized by Poe Dameron as the best recon flier in the force.

FrieTek life support unit

Inflatable life vest

Flight helmet

Snap is said to have a keen eye for trouble and the piloting skill to evade it.

AFTER THE STARKILLER

weapon destroys the New Republic's capital world, Resistance controllers are able to triangulate its location. Snap Wexley flies a daring recon mission into the Unknown Regions, and records vital information about the secret base that allows the Resistance to formulate an attack strategy.

Rebel Roots

The son of Norra Wexley, a veteran Y-wing pilot who flew at the Battle of Endor, Snap hails from Akiva, an Outer Rim world that was an Imperial base prior to its liberation by the New Republic. At that time, young Wexley learned street-smarts and survived with the help of his protector, a modified battle droid named Mister Bones.

SNOWTROOPER

EXTREME-CLIMATE STORMTROOPERS

DATA FILE

AFFILIATION: Empire
SPECIES: Human
HEIGHT: 1.83m (6ft)
STANDARD EQUIPMENT: E-11 blaster rifle; light repeating blasters; grenades
APPEARANCES: V
SEE ALSO: Shock trooper

Polarized snow goggles

IMPERIAL SNOWTROOPERS

are specialized stormtroopers that form self-sufficient mobile combat units in environments of snow and ice. Their backpacks and suit systems keep their bodies warm, while their face masks are equipped with breath heaters.

E-11 blaster rifle

THE EMPIRE modeled its snowtroopers on the Galactic Republic's specialized clone cold assault troopers, who fought in the Clone Wars on frozen worlds such as Orto Plutonia.

Storage pouch

Insulated belt cape

Snowtroopers carry and set up deadly E-web heavy repeating blasters in snowy terrain.

Rugged ice boots

Assault on Hoth

Snowtroopers are deployed as part of General Veers's Blizzard Force at the Battle of Hoth. Snowtroopers work in tandem with AT-AT walkers to effect a massive strike. They defeat the forces of the Rebel Alliance and break into Echo Base. These specialized soldiers can survive for two weeks in extreme cold terrain on suit battery power alone.

SPACE SLUG

GIGANTIC WORMLIKE CREATURES

DATA FILE

HOMEWORLD: Unknown
LENGTH: 10m (33ft)
DIET: Minerals
HABITAT: Asteroids
APPEARANCES: V
SEE ALSO: Han Solo

GIGANTIC EXOGORTHS, otherwise known as space slugs, survive in the airless vacuum of space. They inhabit the nooks and crannies of asteroids. Their wormlike, silicon-based bodies are typically about 10 meters (33 feet) in length, although they can grow to lengths of nearly one kilometer (0.6 mile).

SPACE SLUGS are known to inhabit the Hoth asteroid field. They are actually able to digest minerals from the asteroids on which they live. These solitary, exotic life-forms breed by splitting into two when they reach a certain size. They can then push themselves away from the surface of one asteroid and float through space to land on another.

Teeth for defense

Sensory organs

Space slugs swallow silicon-based mynocks, which live inside their stomachs as parasites.

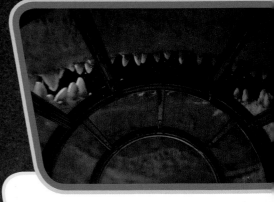

Live Prey

Han Solo unknowingly pilots the *Millennium Falcon* into the stomach of a space slug while escaping the Imperial fleet after the Battle of Hoth. Solo, Chewbacca, and Leia Organa survive inside the space slug with only breath masks to provide oxygen.

STASS ALLIE

THOLOTHIAN JEDI MASTER

DATA FILE

AFFILIATION: Jedi
HOMEWORLD: Tholoth
SPECIES: Tholothian
HEIGHT: 1.8m (5ft 11in)
APPEARANCES: II, III
SEE ALSO: Adi Gallia;
Barriss Offee

Tholoth headdress

Common lightsaber design

THOLOTHIAN Jedi Master Stass Allie serves the Republic during the Clone Wars. As the cousin of a highly distinguished Jedi, Adi Gallia, Allie is keen to demonstrate her own abilities. After Gallia's death in the Clone Wars, Allie takes her place on the Jedi Council.

Utility belt

Stass Allie patrols Saleucami on a speeder bike, where she will lose her life to Order 66.

STASS ALLIE is a formidable warrior, but her talent for healing is even more impressive. Allie passes on her healing expertise to others among the Jedi Order—including Barriss Offee.

Tall travel boots

Brave Fighter

Joining Mace Windu's Jedi task force to Geonosis, Stass Allie participates in the arena battle. She is one of the few survivors, continuing to fight as the battle escalates outside the arena.

STORMTROOPER

THE EMPIRE'S ELITE SOLDIERS

DATA FILE

AFFILIATION: Empire
SPECIES: Human
HEIGHT: 1.83m (6ft)
STANDARD EQUIPMENT:
E-11 blaster rifle; thermal detonator
APPEARANCES: R, IV, V, VI
SEE ALSO: Snowtrooper

STORMTROOPERS ARE THE most effective troops in the Imperial military and the most feared opponents of the Rebel Alliance. They are highly disciplined and completely loyal to the Emperor, carrying out commands without hesitation.

Blaster power cell container

Reinforced alloy plate ridge

STORMTROOPERS

are human recruits who remain anonymous behind their white armor. This armor protects them from harsh environments and glancing shots from blaster bolts.

Sniper position knee protector plate

The massed ranks of disciplined stormtroopers obey their orders unquestioningly.

Fight to Win

In battle, stormtroopers are disciplined to ignore casualties within their own ranks. Notice is only taken from a tactical standpoint. Stormtroopers are never distracted by emotional responses.

Positive-grip boots

STRONO "COOKIE" TUGGS

CASTLE COOK

DATA FILE

AFFILIATION: None
HOMEWORLD: Takodana
SPECIES: Artiodac
HEIGHT: 1.78m (5ft 10in)
Appearances: VII
SEE ALSO: Chewbacca;
Rey; Maz Kanata; Han Solo

STRONO TUGGS'S cooking is the butt of many jokes within Maz Kanata's fortress on Takodana, but they are always said with affection. The grizzled gourmand works hard to keep the castle visitors well fed.

Kitchen
vibro-knife

Stained leather
apron

THE AGED Strono has served for centuries as Maz Kanata's cook, growing increasingly surly with each passing year. He guards his larder and his reputation ferociously, and the wise know better than to make too much fun of his cooking.

Right leg shorter than left

Tough Cookie

Strono challenges the most well-traveled spacers to bring him back any exotic ingredient, which he guarantees he will transform into a tasty meal. When Bobbajo the Crittermonger returned with a giant, tough-skinned megalliform, Strono nearly bit off more than he could chew. After wrestling the enormous fowl into submission, Strono lived up to his word.

UPGRADED BATTLE DROID

DATA FILE

AFFILIATION: Separatists
TYPE: B2 super battle droid
MANUFACTURER: Baktoid Combat Automata
HEIGHT: 1.93m (6ft 4in)
APPEARANCES: II, CW, III
SEE ALSO: Battle droid

Arms stronger than battle droid limbs

Monogrip hands are hard to damage

AFTER THE TRADE FEDERATION'S defeat in the Battle of Naboo, its leaders commissioned an improved battle droid. Tough and heavily armed, super battle droids break Republic regulations on private security forces. However, the Neimoidians have too much influence to care.

THE DROID
foundries of Geonosis secretly manufacture super battle droids. The droids have standard battle droid internal components for economy, but may utilize a much stronger shell.

Flexible armored midsection

Excess heat radiated through calf vanes

Fearless Droids
Super battle droids can be poor at formulating attack plans. However, they make up for this lack by their fearlessness in battle, reducing their targets to ruins.

Strap-on foot tips can be replaced with claws or pads

R2-D2 has his own way of fighting super battle droids: he shoots oil at them, before setting it on fire.

SY SNOOTLES

LEAD VOCALIST FOR THE MAX REBO BAND

DATA FILE

AFFILIATION: Jabba's court
HOMEWORLD: Lowick
SPECIES: Pa'lowick
HEIGHT: 1.6m (5ft 3in)
APPEARANCES: CW, VI
SEE ALSO: Max Rebo; Greeata

Expressive mouth

Retractable tusks protrude from second mouth

Pa'lowicks have lean limbs, round bodies, eye-stalks, and long lip-stalks.

Powerful chest for swimming— and singing!

Skin coloration provides camouflage in swamps of homeworld

SY SNOOTLES IS A Pa'lowick singer and lead vocalist for the Max Rebo Band when they played at Jabba's palace. Snootles only agrees to join the band on the strict condition that Rebo also hires her good friend, Greeata Jendowanian, as a dancer and singer.

SNOOTLES has had an adventurous life. She used to be Ziro the Hutt's lover but then, on discovering the true extent of his cruelty, became his assassin. In Jabba's palace, Snootles works as a double agent, feeding Bib Fortuna's lies to Jabba's enemies.

Microphone stand

Forward and backward-facing toes for walking on shallow lakes

Strange Singing

Jabba's appreciation of Sy Snootles's singing has given her a vastly inflated idea of her own talent. When the band splits up after Jabba's death, Snootles finds it hard to make it anywhere mainstream—the chief reason being her vocals are just too weird.

TARFFUL

WOOKIEE CHIEFTAIN

Teeth bared for war cry

TARFFUL IS LEADER of the Wookiee city of Kachirho. When the Separatist forces invade his planet, Kashyyyk, Tarfful works with Chewbacca and Jedi Yoda, Luminara Unduli, and Quinlan Vos to plan the Wookiees' strategy for repelling the invaders.

Decorative pauldron

Orb-igniter

Tarfful and Chewbacca help Yoda flee in a hidden escape pod after Order 66.

TARFFUL WAS

once enslaved by the Trandoshan slavers, who have long been the enemies of the Wookiees. When clone troops rescued him, Tarfful pledged to fight anyone who tried to enslave his people or capture his planet.

Thick calf muscles from climbing trees

Fur protects upper foot

Wookiee Attack

Tarfful is a calm, considerate Wookiee who can be a mighty warrior when necessary. He leads his fellow Wookiees in daring raids on amphibious Separatist tank droids.

TASU LEECH

TASU LEECH

KANJIKLUB LEADER

DATA FILE

AFFILIATION: Kanjiklub
HOMEWORLD: Nar Kanji
SPECIES: Human
HEIGHT: 1.57m (5ft 2in)
APPEARANCES: VII
SEE ALSO: Chewbacca; Han Solo; rathtar; Razoo Qin-Fee; Kanjiklub gang

TASU LEECH IS the current leader of the notorious Kanjiklub gang. He is an unruly streetfighter who firmly holds on to his position by showing no signs of weakness.

Plastoid blast jerkin

Lightweight armor

Spare ammunition

TASU LEECH

grew up on Nar Kanji, on the frontiers of the galaxy, and clawed his way to the top of the Kanjiklub. He refuses to speak Basic, considering it a weak language of cowardly people.

"Huttsplitter" blaster rifle

Deal Gone Bad

Solo has twice before failed to deliver cargo to Kanjiklub, shortening Tasu's already violent temper. Boarding Han's freighter in search of compensation, Tasu's standoff with Solo turns deadly when a shipment of rathtars escape, sending Kanjiklubbers scurrying for their lives.

TAUNTAUN

HOTH SNOW LIZARDS

DATA FILE

HOMEWORLD: Hoth
HEIGHT: 2m (6.7ft)
DIET: Omnivorous
HABITAT: Snow plains
APPEARANCES: V, VI
SEE ALSO: Luke Skywalker

TAUNTAUNS ARE SNOW LIZARDS that inhabit the ice planet Hoth. They can slow their body functions down to a standstill to survive the intensely cold nights. Tauntauns serve as mounts for the rebel soldiers of Echo Base, who find them more reliable than their patrol vehicles in extreme winds and cold.

Tough lips for scraping lichen

Horns for dominance combat

Saddle

Thick, oily fur

Han Solo uses his dead tauntaun to keep the injured Luke Skywalker warm until help arrives.

Internal organs protected by layers of fat and muscle

TAUNTAUNS

are obedient and hardy mounts but they secrete thick oils and have an unpleasant odor. Patrol riders learn to ignore this, concentrating on the search for signs of Imperial forces.

Missions

Luke Skywalker and Han Solo ride tauntauns on Rebel patrol missions to position a network of life-form sensors along Echo Base's perimeter.

TEEBO

EWOK MYSTIC

DATA FILE

AFFILIATION: Bright Tree Village
HOMEWORLD: Forest moon of Endor
SPECIES: Ewok
HEIGHT: 1.24m (4ft 1in)
APPEARANCES: VI
SEE ALSO: Logray

Churi feathers

Gurreck skull headdress

Teebo joins the Rebel Alliance with his fellow Ewoks to defeat the Imperial army on Endor.

Authority stick

Striped pelt

THE EWOK NAMED Teebo is a watcher of the stars and a poet. Teebo has a mystical connection to the forces of nature. His keen perceptive abilities and practical thinking have made Teebo a leading figure within his tribe.

TEEBO had many adventures growing up in his tribe before becoming an apprentice of the tribal shaman, Logray. He is learning the ways of Ewok magic and hopes to become the Ewok shaman someday.

Aggressive Beginnings

When Teebo first sees Han Solo and his team, he distrusts them. After being freed from his bonds, R2-D2 promptly zaps Teebo's backside!

TEEDO

DATA FILE

AFFILIATION: None
HOMEWORLD: Jakku
SPECIES: Teedo
HEIGHT: 1.24m (4ft 1in)
APPEARANCES: VII
SEE ALSO: luggabeast;
BB-8; Rey

Goggles

TEEDOS ARE SMALL, brutish scavengers that roam the Jakku wilderness, often riding atop cyborg luggabeasts. They scavenge the dunes for salvageable technology and fiercely protect their findings with a tyrannical zeal.

Mag-pulse grenade

Catch bottle recycles bodily fluids

TEEDOS HAVE a peculiar sense of individual identity—the name Teedo seems to identify both the species as a whole and each member within it. Despite their small size, Teedos have an exaggerated sense of their ability to intimidate.

Stealing BB-8

During BB-8's wanderings past Kelvin Ravine in the Jakku wastelands, the droid is snagged in a net by a luggabeast-riding Teedo. A young human scavenger, Rey, shouts down the surly Teedo, convincing the exasperated alien to give up his quarry after he deems the little droid not worth the hassle.

Scaly skin

Sand-shoes cut from droid treads

TESSEK

JABBA'S QUARREN ACCOUNTANT

Hearing organs

Manipulative mouth tentacles

Moisture-retaining robe

TESSEK IS EMPLOYED at Jabba's palace as the Hutt's accountant. But his loyalty to Jabba is a smokescreen. Behind the crime lord's back, Tessek plots to assassinate him and take over his criminal empire. But Tessek does not realize that Jabba probably knows this, too.

TESSEK is a Quarren from Mon Cala. He was involved in galactic politics until the Empire began to enslave his people. This caused Tessek to go into hiding on Tatooine, where he found use for his financial skills among the Hutt gangsters.

Scheming Reputation

Tessek lives up to some of the worst qualities attributed to the Quarren by outsiders. Because of the recurrent civil wars between the Mon Calamari and the Quarren, Quarren have gained the reputation of untrustworthy schemers willing to take any advantage.

TIE FIGHTER PILOT

DATA FILE

AFFILIATION: Empire
SPECIES: Human
STANDARD VEHICLE:
TIE-series starfighters
APPEARANCES: R, IV, V, VI
SEE ALSO: AT-AT pilot

Reinforced
flight helmet

Gas transfer hose

Life support pack

TIE targeting systems and flight
controls are superior to anything
available to rebel fighters.

Vacuum g-suit

TIE FIGHTER PILOTS

form an elite group
within the Imperial navy.
These black-suited pilots
are conditioned to be
entirely dedicated to the
mission and to destroying
their targets, even if this
causes their own deaths.

Energy-shielded fabric

FIGHTER PILOTS take
great pride in their TIE fighters, even
though the ships lack deflector shields
and hyperdrives. The product of
intense training at the Imperial
Academies, TIE pilots are taught they
are the best in the galaxy. As a result,
they are often quite arrogant.

Uniform

The Empire keeps TIE fighter pilots on a
constant state of alert so they are ready for
battle at any time. TIE fighter pilots wear
reinforced flight helmets, with breather tubes
connected to a life support pack. Pilots rely
on their self-contained flight suits to stay
alive in their ships when they are in space.

TION MEDON

PORT ADMINISTRATOR OF PAU CITY

DATA FILE

AFFILIATION: Republic
HOMEWORLD: Utapau
SPECIES: Pau'an
HEIGHT: 2.06m (6ft 9in)
APPEARANCES: III
SEE ALSO: Utai

Utapau's surface is windswept and barren. The Utai and Pau'ans live in cities within huge sinkholes.

TION MEDON IS master of Port Administration for Pau City on Utapau. MagnaGuards kill his committee members and the Separatist leadership use his world as a temporary sanctuary.

Gray, furrowed skin from lack of light in sinkholes

Wide belt supports bony frame

Port master's walking stick

TION MEDON

is a descendent of Timon Medon, who unified Utapau. Like all Pau'ans, Tion prefers darkness to sunlight and raw meat to cooked.

Floor-length robes are a recent fashion

Reassurance

When Jedi Obi-Wan Kenobi lands at Pau City on Utapau, Tion Medon reassures the Jedi that nothing strange has happened. While Kenobi's ship is refueled, Tion whispers that Separatists have taken control of Utapau.

TUSKEN RAIDER

FIERCE TATOOINIAN NOMADS

DATA FILE

AFFILIATION: None
HOMEWORLD: Tatooine
SPECIES: Tusken
HEIGHT: 1.8m (5ft 11in)
APPEARANCES: I, II, IV
SEE ALSO: Bantha

Gaderffii stick made from scavenged metal

Eye-protection lenses

Moisture trap

Thick desert robe

Anakin Skywalker releases his vengeful fury on the Tusken encampment.

TUSKEN RAIDERS, OR

Sand People, are fierce nomads on Tatooine. They compete with human settlers for precious moisture on the desert planet, prowling remote areas, surviving where no others can. Tusken Raiders capture Anakin Skywalker's mother, Shmi, and drag her to their encampment.

SAND PEOPLE

wear heavy clothing to protect them from the planet's harsh suns. They keep their faces hidden behind head bandages. Their traditional weapon is an ax, named a gaderffii (or "gaffi") stick.

Silent Attacker

Sand People are often taller than humans, yet they blend into the landscape with unsettling ease. They sometimes scavenge or steal from the edges of settlement zones. Only the sound of the feared krayt dragon is enough to scare the Sand People away.

During an attack, Tuskens often wield stolen weapons.

UGNAUGHT

PORCINE SPECIES ON CLOUD CITY

DATA FILE

AFFILIATION: None
HOMEWORLD: Gentes
SPECIES: Ugnaught
APPROX. HEIGHT: 1m
(3ft 3in)
APPEARANCES: CW, V, VI
SEE ALSO: Jabba the Hutt

UGNAUGHTS WERE sold into slavery long ago from their home planet Gentes. The eccentric explorer Lord Ecclessis Figg brought in three Ugnaught tribes to help build Cloud City on Bespin. In return, he gave them the freedom of the city.

Tusks used in blood duels

Captain's stripes

AT LEAST one Ugnaught has begun a new life away from Bespin. Yoxgit made a fortune illegally selling tibanna gas to arms dealers, then jumped planet for Tatooine, where he found work with Jabba the Hutt.

Flight gauntlets

Stocky body is efficient at working for long periods

Cloud City Workers

Ugnaught workers in the depths of Cloud City sort through discarded metal junk, where C-3PO nearly ends up after he is blasted to pieces. The species has constructed a network of humid, red-lighted work corridors and tunnels throughout the city, most of which can only be navigated by Ugnaughts.

Ugnaughts perform the often dangerous work of mining and processing tibanna gas.

Expensive tactical boots

UNKAR PLUTT

JUNK BOSS OF JAKKU

DATA FILE

AFFILIATION: None
HOMEWORLD: Unknown
SPECIES: Crolute
HEIGHT: 1.8m (5ft 11in)
APPEARANCES: VII
SEE ALSO: Teedo; Rey;
BB-8

Unkar runs a profitable business stealing, scavenging, and selling scrap on Jakku. He doles out slim servings of food in exchange for valuable salvage, and calls upon leg-breakers and thugs to ensure he gets the best deals.

Bouyant, gelatinous
body tissue

Apron made from
salvaged hull plates

UNKAR OPERATES

out of a converted cargo crawler in a large structure at Niima Outpost. He has a monopoly on food vending in the town, and scavengers are forced to barter with him, exchanging valuable salvage for dehydrated food rations.

Boots conceal
flipper-like limbs

Fish Out of Water

Unkar is an aquatic Crolute, but his greed keeps him far from the oceans of his homeworld and on Jakku, where he reigns as the undisputed junk boss. The scavenger named Rey is one of his favorite traders. When she disappoints him by backing out of a deal, Unkar takes it badly, and sends his goons to teach her a lesson.

UTAI

DATA FILE

AFFILIATION: Republic
HOMEWORLD: Utapau
SPECIES: Utai
HEIGHT: 1.22m (4ft)
APPEARANCES: III
SEE ALSO: Tion Medon

THE HUMBLE AND STOCKY Utai are workers in the sinkholes and caverns of their homeworld, Utapau. They are animal handlers and workers on the various landing platforms. The Utai's prominent eyes give them keen night vision for seeing in the darkness of rock caverns.

Eyes on stalks

LONG AGO, only the Utai lived in Utapau's sinkholes. Later they were joined by Pau'ans from the planet's surface. The Pau'ans and Utai work in harmony, while the primitive Amani settlers stay away from their advanced cities.

Stubby four-fingered hand

Utai mechanics attend to Obi-Wan Kenobi's ship when he lands in Pau City on Utapau.

Varactyl muck boots

Ancient Skills

The Utai's traditional homes are in the crevices of the planet's sinkholes. Long ago, the Utai learned how to domesticate carnivorous, flying dactillions by feeding them fresh meat. They also tamed the varactyl lizards that are used as transport on Utapau, and the Utai still serve as wranglers for the dragon mounts.

VOBER DAND

RESISTANCE GROUND CONTROLLER

DATA FILE

AFFILIATION: Resistance
HOMEWORLD: Suntilla
SPECIES: Tarsunt
HEIGHT: 1.73m (5ft 9 in)
APPEARANCES: VII
SEE ALSO: Nien Nunb; Poe Dameron; Ello Asty; PZ-4CO

Comlink headset

GLD controller's coat

STAYING EVER mobile and out of reach of First Order reprisals, the Resistance uses forgotten bases that were originally built as rebel outposts during the Galactic Civil War. These old, austere facilities ask much from the Resistance's hard-pressed ground personnel.

DURING THE Starkiller crisis, Vober Dand manages the ground crews that maintain the fleet of X-wings at the D'Qar outpost. The hard-nosed Tarsunt runs a tight operation, demanding the best of his teams of mechanics and support staff. Though it's the pilots who get the glory, Dand knows they'd be grounded if not for his efforts.

Logistics Chief

In the loose-knit Resistance organization, Vober Dand holds the rank of chief of Ground Logistics Division. He is one of the first Resistance members consulted when establishing a new base, using his mathematical mind to calculate the specifics of flight schedules, maintenance requirements, and hangar operations.

Without the deep finances and government supplies of the New Republic, Vober Dand must keep the Resistance's small fleet of X-wings flying at all hours.

WAMPA

RAVENOUS ICE CREATURES

DATA FILE

HOMEWORLD: Hoth
HEIGHT: 3m (9ft 10in)
DIET: Carnivorous
HABITAT: Snow plains
APPEARANCES: CW, V
SEE ALSO: Tauntaun

Curving horns

Fanged mouth

Thick white fur for insulation and camouflage

Razor-sharp claws

HUGE WAMPA ICE creatures hunt tauntauns and other beasts on the snow plains of Hoth, where their howling wails blend with the icy winds at night. They are normally solitary beasts but have been known to band together to make raids on human settlements. Wampas often attack the rebel base on Hoth.

Hungry Beast

Wampas sate their hunger on freshly killed tauntaun meat. Human flesh is relatively unknown to wampas, but highly prized.

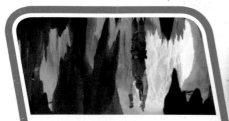

Luke Skywalker returns to consciousness hanging upside down in a wampa cave.

WAMPAS' SHAGGY

white fur provides warmth and camouflage in the snowy conditions of Hoth. These cunning predators stalk their prey before lunging at it, using their powerful arms to stun it.

WAT TAMBOR

EMIR AND FOREMAN OF THE TECHNO UNION

Darth Vader shows no mercy to Wat Tambor on Mustafar.

Vocabulator/annunciator

Dials control vocabulator

Rich outer tunic over pressure suit

WAT TAMBOR IS FOREMAN of the Techno Union, a powerful commercial body that makes massive profits from new technologies. He is also an Executive of arms manufacturer, Baktoid Armor Workshop.

TAMBOR LEFT his home planet Skako at an early age and began a career in technology on the harsh industrial world of Metalorn. Few Skakoans leave their world due to its unique atmospheric pressure. In fact, Tambor must wear a special suit to avoid his body exploding in standard, oxygen-based atmospheres.

Raiding Ryloth

During the Clone Wars, Tambor oversees the sacking of Ryloth, homeworld of the Twi'leks. Tambor and his droid army hold the capital city, Lessu, until they are pushed out during a counterattack by General Mace Windu. Tambor is then captured and imprisoned.

WATTO

TOYDARIAN JUNK DEALER

WATTO IS A QUICK-WITTED, flying Toydarian shopkeeper who owns a spare parts business in Mos Eisley on Tatooine. He has a sharp eye for a bargain and spends his proceeds at podraces, gambling with Hutts, and winning slaves—including Anakin and Shmi Skywalker.

DATA FILE

AFFILIATION: None
HOMEWORLD: Toydaria
SPECIES: Toydarian
HEIGHT: 1.37m (4ft 6in)
APPEARANCES: I, II
SEE ALSO: Qui-Gon Jinn; Anakin Skywalker; Shmi Skywalker

Flexible, trunk-like nose

Three-day stubble

WATTO was a soldier on his homeworld Toydaria, but left the planet after suffering an injury. On Tatooine, he watched how the Jawas sold used goods, learning some of their tricks before setting up his own business.

Large belly mostly composed of gas

Keycodes for main safe and slave keepers

Watto insists his shop is a parts dealership, though most call it a junkshop.

Watto is surprised that his former slave, Anakin Skywalker, is now a Jedi.

Chance Meeting

When Watto meets an off-worlder looking for spare hyperdrive parts, he sees an opportunity for some profitable swindling. Jedi Qui-Gon Jinn does not suspect that he will meet the prophesied Chosen One, Anakin Skywalker, in this very shop. Losing Anakin to the Jedi is the start of a downward spiral for Watto, who eventually loses his other slave, Shmi, too.

WICKET W. WARRICK

YOUNG EWOK LONER

DATA FILE

AFFILIATION: Bright Tree Village

HOMEWORLD: Forest moon of Endor

SPECIES: Ewok

HEIGHT: 80cm (2ft 7in)

APPEARANCES: VI

SEE ALSO: Princess Leia; Teebo; Logray; Chief Chirpa

Spear

Hood

Thick fur

Wicket's knowledge of the forest assists the rebels in their attack on the Imperial forces.

WICKET W. WARRICK

is a young Ewok with a reputation as a loner. He spends much time wandering far from his village in the forests of Endor's moon. Wicket is on one of his travels when he runs into Princess Leia Organa. He helps her to the safety of his treetop village, and soon comes to trust her.

YOUNG Wicket had an adventurous childhood with his great friends—Teebo, Kneesaa, Paploo, and his brothers Weechee and Willy. Though Wicket respects the mystic shamanic magic employed by Logray, he does not possess the patience to practise it.

Friends?

Wicket bonds with Leia, and when her friends arrive, he argues that they should be spared any abuse. But his solitary habits leave him with a big lack of influence among the elders in his Bright Tree village.

X-WING PILOTS

DATA FILE

AFFILIATION: Rebel Alliance
SPECIES: Human
STANDARD VEHICLE: X-wing starfighter
APPEARANCES: IV, V, VI
SEE ALSO: Luke Skywalker

Life-support unit

Alliance symbol

Insulated helmet

Equipment pocket

Gear harness

MANY X-WING pilots of Red Squadron become legendary figures in the Rebel Alliance. Pilots such as Biggs Darklighter ("Red Three"), Wedge Antilles ("Red Two"), and Luke Skywalker ("Red Five") are crucial to the destruction of the first Death Star.

RED SQUADRON fly T-65 X-wing starfighters. These ships are equipped with droid sockets for astromech droids, long-range laser cannons, and a small payload of proton torpedoes.

Wedge Antilles

A native of Corellia, Wedge Antilles is one of just two X-wing pilots (the other being Luke Skywalker) who survive the Battle of Yavin, in which the Empire's Death Star is destroyed. Antilles flies a snowspeeder at the Battle of Hoth, and is the leader of Red Squadron at the Battle of Endor.

Luke's childhood friend Biggs Darklighter takes part in the assault on the first Death Star.

YADDLE

COMPASSIONATE JEDI MASTER

DATA FILE

AFFILIATION: Jedi
HOMEWORLD: Unknown
SPECIES: Unknown
HEIGHT: 61cm (2ft)
APPEARANCES: 1
SEE ALSO: Yoda;
Oppo Rancisis

SITTING ON THE Jedi High Council, Master Yaddle offers few words but much compassion and balanced patience. She looks up to Master Yoda, who is of the same species as her but is almost twice her age (Yaddle is a mere 477!). Yaddle has trained many Jedi Padawans, including fellow Council member Oppo Rancisis.

Mind and Body

Yaddle has devoted a lot of time to scholarly interests, and spends much time in the Jedi archives. But she has been an active Jedi in the field, too.

YADDLE is one of the few Jedi permitted to practice morichro. This ancient art enables the user to rapidly slow down an opponent's bodily functions to the point of death.

Youthful topknot

Shapely ears

YARAEL POOF

QUERMIAN JEDI MASTER

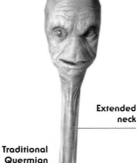

DATA FILE

AFFILIATION: Jedi
HOMEWORLD: Quermia
SPECIES: Quermian
HEIGHT: 2.64m (8ft 8in)
APPEARANCES: I
SEE ALSO: Obi-Wan Kenobi;
Qui-Gon Jinn

Extended
neck

Traditional
Quermian
cannom collar

JEDI MASTER Yarael Poof is a member of the High Council at the time of the Naboo crisis. He is a master of specialized Jedi mind tricks, which he can use to bring conflicts to a decisive end.

Deceptive Appearances

Yarael Poof quietly watches the proceedings as Qui-Gon Jinn and Obi-Wan Kenobi report from their mission to Naboo. Though appearing as a serene thinker among the Jedi Council members, Master Yarael is a dexterous combatant with a lightsaber, and has perfected many incredible moves that only his spineless anatomy can allow.

Poof has a mischievous side and enjoys playing mind tricks on colleagues.

QUERMIANS have extended necks and long limbs, as well as a second pair of arms, which Poof hides under his Jedi robe. The species is noseless, as Quermians smell with olfactory glands in their hands. They also have two brains—an upper brain in the head and a lower brain in the chest.

Robe hides
second pair of
arms and chest
with lower brain

YARNA

ASKAJIAN DANCER AT JABBA'S PALACE

DATA FILE

AFFILIATION: Jabba's court
HOMEWORLD: Askaji
SPECIES: Askajian
HEIGHT: 1.73m (5ft 8in)
APPEARANCES: VI
SEE ALSO: Jabba the Hutt;
Oola

Makeup hides
Yarna's true beauty

Body enlarged to
resemble a Hutt

YARNA D'AL' GARGAN has been a dancer at Jabba's palace for many years. The daughter of an Askajian tribal chief, Yarna was captured by slavers and transported to Tatooine, where Jabba bought her. Jabba's cruel whim is to force Yarna to wear special makeup to make her look more like his mother.

Yarna performs highly exotic dances for Jabba's pleasure.

ON ASKAJI Yarna had
been married with four siblings.
She and her husband danced for
her tribe. When taken by slavers,
and her family, she lost her
husband. Nullage in. Yarna
for insubordination, and kept the
cublings in his Mos Eisley warehouse.

Better Future

Yarna hates Jabba, but has become close to some of the palace regulars. After the Hutt's death, Yarna escapes his hated palace and is reunited with her precious cublings.

YODA

LEGENDARY JEDI MASTER

DATA FILE

AFFILIATION: Jedi
HOMEWORLD: Unknown
SPECIES: Unknown
HEIGHT: 66cm (2ft 2in)
APPEARANCES: I, II, CW, III, R, V, VI
SEE ALSO: Luke Skywalker

Head has been nearly bald for centuries

YODA IS ONE OF THE most powerful Jedi ever, and has lived to be nearly 900 years old. He served the Galactic Republic at its height, as well as through its decline and fall. Yoda is one of the few Jedi to survive the Clone Wars—he goes into hiding on the remote planet Dagobah.

Homespun robe

YODA HAS

guided hundreds of Jedi to knighthood and visited countless worlds. He takes quiet satisfaction in his ability to resolve conflict by nonviolent means, until the re-emergence of the dark side unseats others' confidence in him.

Sith Fury

Accepting finally that the Clone Wars have been nothing more than a manipulation by the Sith to destroy the Jedi Order, Yoda confronts Palpatine. Even the diminutive Jedi's amazing strength and speed, however, are not a match for the devastating fury of a Sith Lord.

On Dagobah, Yoda trains Luke Skywalker, his final student and the galaxy's last hope.

Anakin, Yoda, and Obi-Wan become one with the Force after their deaths.

ZAM WESELL

DATA FILE

AFFILIATION: Bounty hunter
HOMEWORLD: Zolan
SPECIES: Clawdite
HEIGHT: 1.68m
(5ft 6in)
APPEARANCES: II
SEE ALSO: Jango Fett

KYD-21
blaster

ZAM WESELL is a hired assassin with a special edge. As a Clawdite shape-shifter, Wesell can change her appearance to mimic that of other species. For some years, Zam has worked with renowned bounty hunter Jango Fett.

Bodysuit stretches to
allow shape-shifting

Direct-to-lungs
breathpack

Blast-energy skirt

ZAM WESELL

was born on Zolan, the home of the Mabari, an ancient order of warrior-knights. The Mabari trained Zam until her desire for wealth took her to the vast metropolis of Denon, where she employed her skills and training as an assassin.

Airspeeder Chase

Zam Wesell often steals a new vehicle for each job, to avoid being traced. But she uses her own airspeeder when she knows she needs to get away fast. When Zam takes on a job for Jango Fett—to kill Senator Padmé Amidala—she has to outrun two Jedi Knights in a borrowed speeder who are hard on her trail.

Boots accept
a variety of
limb forms

In her true Clawdite form, Zam Wesell is a reptilian humanoid.

ZUCKUSS

GAND BOUNTY HUNTER

DATA FILE

AFFILIATION: Bounty hunter
HOMEWORLD: Gand
SPECIES: Gand
HEIGHT: 1.5m (4ft 11in)
APPEARANCES: V
SEE ALSO: 4-LOM

Compound eyes

Ammonia respirator

Heavy battle armor under robe

Breather packs

Findsman body cloak

ZUCKUSS IS an insectoid Gand bounty hunter who often partners with droid bounty hunter 4-LOM. Zuckuss is a tireless tracker, who uses the mystic findsman traditions that date back centuries on his fog-shrouded homeworld, Gand.

ZUCKUSS breathes only ammonia, so he wears a respirator in oxygen-based atmospheres. When his planet's findsman traditions began dying out, Zuckuss became one of the first findsmen to go off-world. Bounty hunting is now a lucrative way for him to use his particular talents.

Zuckuss is renowned for his tracking skills and is a highly sought-after bounty hunter.

Powerful Pair

Zuckuss's uncanny abilities make other bounty hunters uneasy. But not 4-LOM, whom Zuckuss partners with many times. The two bounty hunters make a formidable team. The pairing does not go unnoticed by Darth Vader, who hires them to locate the *Millennium Falcon*.

INDEX

ACKNOWLEDGMENTS

Penguin Random House

Project Editor David Fentiman
Editors Jo Casey, Matt Jones, Arushi Vats
Senior Designer Clive Savage
Project Art Editor Owen Bennett
Assistant Art Editor Akansha Jain
Designer Jon Hall
Additional Design Sandra Perry, Dan Bunyan, Rhys Thomas,
Toby Truphet, Lynne Moulding
DTP Designers Umesh Singh Rawat, Rajdeep Singh
Pre-Production Manager Sunil Sharma
Pre-Production Producer Marc Staples
Senior Producer Alex Bell
Managing Editors Sadie Smith, Chitra Subramanyam
Managing Art Editors Neha Ahuja, Ron Stobbart
Art Director Lisa Lanzarini
Publisher Julie Ferris
Publishing Director Simon Beecroft

For Lucasfilm
Executive Editor Jonathan W. Rinzler
Story Group Pablo Hidalgo, Leland Chee, Rayne Roberts
Image Archives Tina Mills, Stacey Leong, Matthew Azeveda,
Shahana Alam
Art Director Troy Alders

Dorling Kindersley would like to thank Elizabeth Dowsett, Joel Kempson, Julia March,
and Lisa Stock for editorial assistance, and Anne Sharples for design assistance.

First American Edition, 2011
This edition published in the United States in 2016 by
DK Publishing, 345 Hudson Street,
New York, New York 10014
DK, a Division of Penguin Random House LLC

Page Design Copyright © 2016 Dorling Kindersley Limited

16 17 18 19 20 10 9 8 7 6 5 4 3 2 1

001-280563-04/16

A catalog record for this book is available from the Library of Congress.
ISBN 978-1-4654-4885-9

DK books are available at special discounts when purchased in bulk for sales
promotions, premiums, fund-raising, or educational use. For details, contact:
DK Publishing Special Markets, 345 Hudson Street, New York, New York 10014
SpecialSales@dk.com

Printed and bound in China

www.dk.com
www.starwars.com

A WORLD OF IDEAS:
SEE ALL THERE IS TO KNOW